A Prayer for
America

A PRAYER FOR
AMERICA

DENNIS KUCINICH

PREFACE BY STUDS TERKEL

THUNDER'S MOUTH PRESS/NATION BOOKS

NEW YORK

*For my dear daughter Jacqueline, whose clarity and humor
embodies the passion of the next generation*

PRAYER FOR AMERICA

Published by
Thunder's Mouth Press/Nation Books
245 West 17th St., 11th Fl
New York, NY 10011

Nation Books is a co-publishing venture of the Nation Institute and
Avalon Publishing Group Incorporated.

Library of Congress Cataloging-in-Publication Data is available.

ISBN 1-56025-510-2

9 8 7 6 5 4 3 2 1

Book design by
Printed in the United States of America
Distributed by Publishers Group West

CONTENTS

PREFACE
KUCINICH IS THE ONE

STUDS TERKEL

When I finished reading John Nichols's exhilarating communiqué from California, "Kucinich Rocks the Boat," in the March 25, 2002 issue of *The Nation,* the bells began to ring. In his speech to the Southern California Americans for Democratic Action, criticizing Bush's conduct of the war on terrorism, Dennis Kucinich set the crowd on its ear—one standing ovation after another. Sure, they were all liberals, but what counted was the response on the Internet. The Cleveland congressman's e-mail box was stuffed to overflowing with twenty-thousand-plus enthusiastic letters. Among them was the call: Kucinich for President. That's when—bingo!—I remembered my first encounter with him. It was twenty-four years ago.

At the arrival gate of the Chicago-to-Cleveland flight, a skinny kid who appeared no more than nineteen or twenty reached out for my torn duffel bag. I thought he was one of those Horatio Alger heroes, whose opening line is usually "Smash your baggage, mister?" This one said, "Did you have a good flight, Studs?" I'll be damned, he was the person I had come to visit, Dennis Kucinich, the Boy Mayor of Cleveland.

He was thirty-two then, though he could pass as anybody's office boy. As he carried my bag through the corridors of the airport, passers-by called out, "Hello, Mr. Mayor." I was slightly discombobulated, turning around several times to make sure whom they were addressing. The following are passages from our conversation in 1978.

At his one-family bungalow, his wife makes coffee. A player piano is about the only piece of furniture that might distinguish the house from any other simply furnished home in this working-class neighborhood. "Some of my neighbors are within ten years of retirement." A photograph of Thomas Jefferson, in the shadows, hangs on the wall.

When I was young, I never dreamed of living in a house like this. We were always renters. A number of times we moved; it was because we were kicked out. It wasn't for failure to pay rent. It was because our family was big. I remember sometimes, in order to get a place, one of the kids had to be hid in the closet. We always lived above some railroad tracks.

I'm the oldest of seven. There were a lot of tough times. My father came from a family of thirteen children, my mother from a family of a dozen. Our story is an ethnic *Gone with the Wind. (Laughs)*

I spent all my time as a youngster coming to understand the experience of the ghetto. It was growing up tough and growing up absurd. I spent a lot of time out on the streets. That's where I got my education. I made friends with all kinds of people, black and white.

My dad's been a truck driver ever since he got out of the service as a marine. He's gung ho. His dream was to have all his boys in the marines. My brother Frank served four years, two and a half in Vietnam. My brother Gary served five years, most of it in Hawaii. My father never questioned authority. His authority was the guy who ran the trucking company.

I've always been taught to respect authority, although I was more independent than the other kids my age. I was constantly getting into squabbles with teachers. I was the first person in my family, on both sides, who ever graduated from college. I love literature. My mother taught me to read when I was three.

In the late sixties, I didn't go right from high school to college. I worked for two and a half years. When I was seventeen, I moved on my own and rented an apartment above the steel mills. In the same neighborhood where *The Deer Hunter* was filmed. The frame house I lived in overlooked the steel mills.

When I was in grade school, I would scrub floors and help with janitorial duties to pay my tuition. When I got into high school, I worked as a caddy at the country club, from 1959 to '64. I was carrying two bags. They called it workin' doubles. Going forty-five holes a day, six days a week.

I believe in the work ethic. There's a tremendous dignity in work, and it doesn't matter what it is. What some consider menial, I found to be just a chance to make a living. I always tried to do the best I could at that time. Work hard, get ahead—that was my American dream.

We lived next door to black people. It was integrated. There's a lot of poor and working ethnics who have to struggle their way into the system, who can identify with black people's striving. I'm trying to show both that the color of the enemy is green. (*Laughs*) This is a city run by the Mayflower-type aristocracy. It's as if the people here don't even exist. Until recently. We seized the decision-making power through the ballot box. If the black movement did one thing, it created ethnic pride.

I'd ask myself why it is that with so many people trying to improve society, not that much changes. As I looked around, I saw many of the kids I grew up with trapped, not able to get as far as they would have liked. I started to wonder, *What the heck is this?* No matter how hard they work, they can't get ahead. Seeing all these people working their heads off, you find out the system is rigged.

When I first started, I didn't question the institutions. I never really put it together. I think it was the

Vietnam War. I'd see that some people were profiting, while tens of thousands of Americans were dying. Friends of mine went over there and they died. Kids I rode the bus with to school. I started to think, *This is a dirty business. I'd better start to find out more about it.*

I began to get into city politics. In 1967, I ran for the city council. I was twenty-one. I went from door to door, and I found out about people. Every campaign I've ever run has been door to door. I spent months just talking to people. They don't ask for much, but they don't get anything. They can have a problem with a streetlight that's out, with a street that's caved in, with a fire hydrant that's leaking, with flooded basements, with snow that isn't plowed.

I've visited tens of thousands of homes over the past years. That's how I got my real education. Door to door.

I was elected councilman in '69. I had just turned twenty-three. My ward was made up of Polish, Ukrainians, Russians, Greeks, Slovaks, Appalachians, Puerto Ricans, blacks. It was a good cross section not only of Cleveland but of America. They worked in the mills around here. Some had lived in the neighborhood sixty years. Same homes. The churches are still here. They say masses in Polish and Slovak and Russian. They helped keep the neighborhood alive. I loved it.

People were wondering how the heck I got elected to the council. No one believed the old councilman could ever be beaten, he was so entrenched. At first, people wondered if the banks sent me there. Or the utilities. Or

some big real estate interests. All the traditional contrib-
utors who buy their candidates. I was elected on a shoe-
string. I financed nearly my whole campaign out of my
pocket, my savings, which weren't much. I put together
a coalition of people who were disaffected and ignored.

The first thing, some of the older guys came up to
me and said, "You got it made now, kid. All you have
to do is take your seat and shut up. If you just listen to
what we tell you, you're gonna be a big man in this
town someday."

When I started stepping on toes, I didn't know I was
stepping on toes. I was just representing the people who
sent me to the city council. I didn't know I was
offending somebody else. I found out very quickly there
were a number of special-interest groups who made City
Hall their private warren. There are thirty-three coun-
cilmen. Thirty-two to one was usually the score.

When I got elected mayor, just as I came to the
council, I was expected to represent the system. When
I started to challenge it, the titans of Cleveland's business community began to get surly and used their
clout in the media to disparage the administration. I
came to understand that big business has a feudal view
of the city, and that City Hall was within their fiefdom.

When I was elected mayor on November 8, 1977, it
was discovered that the previous administration had
misspent tens of millions of dollars of bond funds.
They could not be accounted for. The city was trying
to negotiate the renewal of $14 million worth of notes

held in local banks. One bank balked: the Cleveland
Trust Company.

I had a meeting on the day of default at eight o'clock
in the morning with the council president, the chairman
of the board of Cleveland Trust, and a local businessman,
a friend of mine. The conversation turned immediately
to MUNY Light. The chairman of the board of Cleveland
Trust made it very clear that if I sold MUNY Light to the
Cleveland Electric Illuminating Company, he would
extend credit and save the city from default. CEI's largest
shareholder is Cleveland Trust. Four members of Cleveland Trust's board are directors of CEI. If I didn't agree, I
could not expect any help from his bank.

MUNY Light has 46,000 customers in Cleveland.
MUNY Light and CEI compete in most neighborhoods, street by street, house by house. MUNY Light's
rates in the recent decades have been from 20 to 30
percent cheaper than CEI's, but MUNY Light's competitive advantage has depreciated over the years
because of CEI's interference in MUNY's management.

From the moment Mr. Weir (Brock Weir, chairman
of the board of CEI) told me his price, I decided that a
fiscal default was better than a moral default. If I had
cooperated with them and sold MUNY Light to the
private utility, everyone's electric rates would've auto-
matically gone up. It would have set the stage for
never-ending increases, much the same way that Fort
Wayne, Indiana, is faced with that problem after relin-
quishing its rights to a municipal electric system.

I was hoping I was doing the right thing in holding my ground. I had to tell 'em no. I felt they were trying to sell the city down the river. They were trying to blackmail me. If I went along with the deal, they made it clear, things would be easy. Mr. Weir said he'd put together $50 million of new credit for the city. The financial problems would be solved. My term as mayor would be comfortable and the stage set for future cooperation between myself and the business community.

The media picked up the tempo. "Why the heck don't you get rid of MUNY Light?" I was asked on a live TV show. I replied that MUNY Light was a false issue. It wasn't losing money. Its troubles could be traced to CEI's interference. I was in office a little over a year and had inherited a mess. The city had a plan to avoid default, to which five of the six banks agreed: an income-tax increase, as well as tighter control of the management of the city's money. I knew I was risking my whole political career. But you gotta stand for something.

The referendum was to be on February 27. Both issues were on the ballot: the income-tax increase and the sale of MUNY Light. We organized volunteers. People went door-to-door, in the freezing rain and the bitter cold, subzero temperatures, and big snow. We laid out the hard facts. We were facing the attempt of corporations to run the city. We gave the people a choice between a duly elected government and an un-duly unelected shadow government.

We were outspent two and a half to one, but we

created circumstances where people came to understand that every person can make a difference. We won both issues by about two to one. It was the first time in Cleveland's history that we succeeded in uniting whites and blacks, poor and middle class, on economic issues. Usually, they've been manipulated against each other. Not this time.

My concept of the American dream? It's not the America of IBM, ITT, and Exxon. It's the America of Paine and Jefferson and Samuel Adams. There are increasingly two Americas: the America of multinationals dictating decisions in Washington, and the America of neighborhoods and rural areas, who feel left out. I see, in the future, a cataclysm: popular forces converging on an economic elite, which feels no commitments to the needs of the people. That clash is already shaping up.

The American Revolution never really ended. It's a continuing process. I think we're approaching the revolution of hope. We have the country that makes it possible for people, if they've lost control of the government, to regain it in a peaceful way; Through the ballot box. Before I got into politics, I didn't know whether what I was doing even mattered. Now I know. One person can make a difference. I think it's something every person can learn. The main thing is, you can't be afraid.

In November 1979, with just about all of Cleveland's newspapers and television and radio stations—as well as industry—united against him, Kucinich was defeated for reelection. Fifteen years later, he began his political come-back, elected to the Ohio Senate. His key issue: expanding Cleveland's municipal electrical system, which provided low-cost power to almost half the residents of Cleveland. In 1988, the Cleveland City Council honored him for "having the courage and foresight to refuse to sell the city's municipal electric system." It was the same political body that in years past outvoted him thirty-two to one.

Today, in his second term as a U.S. congressman from Ohio, he is chairman of the Progressive Caucus, and its spark plug. His website reads like a press release: "He combines a powerful political activism with a spiritual sense of the interconnectedness of all living things. His holistic worldview carries with it a passionate commit-ment to public service, peace, human rights, workers' rights, and the environment. His advocacy of a Depart-ment of Peace seeks not only to make nonviolence an organizing principle in our society, but to make war archaic." This sounds naïve and loonily idealistic, except for one thing: He is a remarkably practical and astute politician. His Ohio track record tells you that.

It was his voice in the state senate that caused Ohio to scrap the planned siting of a nuclear waste dump in the state. He gets things done in no small way because of his understanding of his opponents' humanness as well as his wrongness. There is an ultraconservative congressman from a nearby state whom Kucinich describes as a "good, honest man." I spoke to that congressman and discovered that he admires Dennis very much. You get the idea? I think this guy can reach anyone and change seemingly unchangeable minds.

It's more than a hunch that tells me Kucinich Is the One (if I may borrow a Nixonian slogan). I am a believer in egalitarianism, and I feel it's high time an Ohioan had another shot at the presidency. We've had only three since the eminently forgettable Rutherford B. Hayes in 1876.

In 1896, Ohio gave us William McKinley, with a little help from his boss, Mark Hanna. In 1908, it gave us William Howard Taft, fondly remembered as the heaviest occupant in the history of the White House. And in 1920, we were gifted with the genial, handsome, presidential-looking Warren Gamaliel Harding. Even though I was only eight at the time, I remember it with some sense of pride because his nomination happened in my hometown, Chicago. In a smoke-filled room at the Blackstone Hotel, the Boys, blowing wondrous smoke rings from H. Upmanns, with a touch of bourbon or two to lift all spirits, boozily announced that Harding was the one. Sure, he was as little known, say, as Dennis Kucinich, but with the leading candidates, General Leonard Wood and Governor Frank Lowden in a damn deadlock, they said, What the hell, here's a good-lookin' guy. And we gotta get home.

Now, in the year 2002, Ohio has given us another, of a somewhat different stripe. I doubt whether he'll ever make *People* magazine's list of the most beautiful people, but the blue-collar Kucinich is the only one who can win back the blue-collar Reagan Democrats, among the other disenchanted, and the disfranchised. He talks the language they understand and, at fifty-five, with remarkable eloquence.

Imagine him in a televised, coast-to-coast debate with Dubya. Blood wouldn't flow, but it would be a knockout in the first round, and we'd have an honest-to-God working-class president for the first time in our history. It's a crazy thought, of course, but it's quite possible, considering the roller-coaster nature of our times.

Since plagiarism is à la mode these days, let me steal the closing passage from the Reverend William Sloane Coffin's invocation at a Yale commencement during the Vietnam War: "Oh God, take our minds and think through them, take our lips and speak through them, take our hearts and set them on fire." I'll add a brief benediction: Kucinich is the man to light the fire. Amen.

Postscript. Obviously, I haven't touched on ways and means. Obviously, the big dough will not be there. But this could be the catapult for the hundreds of grassroots groups on a thousand and one issues to coalesce behind one banner. Jim Hightower has touched on that often. And Michael Moore's book *Stupid White Men* is a bestseller. And there's a whole new generation of kids, not just the students, but bewildered, lost blue-collar kids. And, strangely enough, it can be done the old-fashioned way, shoe leather and bell-ringing, as well as e-mail. It could be that exciting. Nicholas von Hoffman once observed that when people get active, they get the feeling they count. Kucinich is like Poe's purloined letter—right there on the table as we helplessly play Inspector Clouseau goofily searching elsewhere.

VISIONS

CLEVELAND: A NATIONAL LABORATORY

The 1977 mayoral election turned Cleveland into a national political laboratory, by way of shifting power from corporations, banks, utilities, and real estate trusts, to poor and working people. It put to test a significant political question: "Can a city government, based on the support of the poor and working people, increase services to improve the standard of living and quality of life, and survive politically without the support of big business and even with active opposition?" In Cleveland, we believe the answer is "Yes." We are dedicated to championing the economic rights of poor and working people.

As our city administration has striven to improve quality of life in Cleveland, we've met resistance from the corporate sector. Big business found that City Hall no longer rubber-stamped the demands of power brokers. It soon became obvious to certain members of Cleveland's business elite that our administration was an obstacle. In siding with poor and working people on economic issues, we found ourselves locked in mortal combat with every mighty institution in Cleveland. Conventional wisdom would have you believe that no one can win and hold elective office without support from the business establishment, and the help of political parties, or in the face of unrelenting opposition from the media.

The establishment is accustomed to winning all elections. When they don't succeed in electing their preferred candidate, they readily co-opt the winner into their preferred circle. But what if he won't make book? An elected official who has no price is too dangerous to be permitted to survive. Virtually the day after my narrow November victory, big business hitched a ride on a recall petition drive spearheaded by sore losers, discharged political hacks, and corrupt interests who are no longer welcome at City Hall. Throughout the recall, no charges of corruption or even allegations of wrongdoing were leveled at our administration. Nevertheless, it became the civic project of city power brokers, the business elite, political parties, three local television stations, five radio stations, and three major newspapers.

The news media's advocacy of the recall illustrated the dangerous intersection between media and corporate interests. The local media overpowered freedom of expression and presented a contrived consensus of distorted alleged facts adverse to the political and economic interests of ordinary citizens.

Economic democracy is a condition of political democracy. The defense of economic rights of the weak is an essential part of renewing the great spirit of our nation. We must firmly establish a political agenda based on economic justice for each and every individual. Big business, big government, and big media are all out of touch with mainstream America. They do not know how thoroughly disappointed, utterly disgusted, and fed up ordinary people are. They are unaware how readily myths can be toppled.

In Cleveland and around the country, a new movement is emerging. New urban populism is uniting poor and working people, both black and white, on economic issues. We're improving the working man's ability to retain income, and resisting government's continuous tendency to increase taxes. We have not, nor will we, increase taxes. We're making sure that big business pays its fair share of taxes. When big business pays taxes, government is better able to collect the revenues necessary to maintain services. New urban populism is rooted in a philosophy of responsiveness and accountability. It derives strength from direct contact with the people. All too often, citizens of major cities are deprived of close relationships with their governments. I begin the first hour of each day taking phone calls from the general public to gauge the effectiveness of the city's service delivery and the overall responsiveness of government. My cabinet, city directors, and commissioners are involved in a continuous door-to-door canvass of the city's neighborhoods to make government more accessible than ever and to take people's complaints and listen to their suggestions.

The stakes at the municipal level are high. The interests

of the public sector and the private sector are often mutually exclusive. No one understands this better than big business. So in response, in Cleveland we required big business to pay a fair share of property taxes. We stood up to corporate extortionists who threaten to pull up stakes unless the city capitulates to millions of dollars of property tax abatements. By refusing tax concessions to commercial developers, we stopped the shift of taxation from those who are best able to pay onto those homeowners for whom property tax rates are becoming confiscatory.

Consumers have a stake in the fight against utility monopolies. We rescued a municipal electric system from the clutches of one of America's most profitable privately owned utilities, the Cleveland Electric Illuminating Company. We revived the prosecution of a $325 million antitrust damage suit against the same utility, for unfair and anti-competitive practices, which have been confirmed in findings by the Nuclear Regulatory Commission. We are continuing to maintain municipal utilities because we believe, as former Cleveland mayor, Tom Johnson, once said, that public service facilities must belong to the public. They are not to be considered private loot. They are public rights. Our defense of our municipal electric utility assures Cleveland consumers of the advantages of continued competition and provides them with an alternative for lower electric rates. Our urban populism brought about a twenty-five-cent bus fare and sharply limited developers' schemes for fixed rail expansion into Northern Ohio's cornfields.

We have escalated efforts aimed at getting local banks to eliminate discriminatory lending policies. We're enforcing air and water pollution laws, a policy which puts us at odds with the wealthiest industries in the community. We're breaking the hold of the police department on the city's political process, which we believe will ultimately produce a community-responsive police. We're resisting the gimmick of county-wide government, which reduces the influence of city residents in determining their city's destiny.

American cities in the Midwest and Northeast are urgently in need of government policies which seek to arrest the abuse of the concentrated power that creates problems like the runaway shop. In the last decade, thousands of companies have shut down their facilities in the Northeast and Midwest or drastically cut back operations. These privately controlled companies seek low wages, no unions, and tax giveaways. They allege that they are looking for the amenities of the Sunbelt; in truth they want nothing more than a docile labor force and a free ride. They don't care how their decisions impact communities; their primary concern is making a profit. I don't object to the development of industry in the South, but I do object to corporations playing Northern cities against the Sunbelt. I object to companies rejecting social responsibility and casting aside the lives of tens of thousands of our residents. What we need is national legislation that forces companies to announce place relocations years ahead of time, contribute financially to cities they abandon, and stop the federal government from giving tax breaks that encourage companies to move.

We accept as gospel the outrageous trade-off of higher unemployment for more stable prices. Do we seriously believe we have no other alternatives? If we have no choice but recession or inflation then we are admitting that the free enterprise system is a failure. Inflation can be controlled through limitations on profits that business derives from higher prices. Inflation must ultimately be addressed as the greatest consumer fraud of our time. Price increases aim to maximize profits and inflation is a wonderful excuse. We debate endlessly whether wage and price guidelines can be effective without actual control of whether controls are essential.

You may notice that I haven't touched on any of the great debates over social issues. Trifling with social issues evades our responsibility to face economic issues, diminishing the potential for economic issues to rally popular support. The basis of genuine reform is economic reform. We can solve economic problems if we refuse to be distracted. The failure is one of courage among reformers to attempt to mobilize popular support for basic economic issues, which challenge the economic interests of big business. The substitution of social issues in place of economic issues (far from offering an alternative route to progressive policies) trifles with people's problems, and offers false solutions such as the integration of schools which are so bad that you wouldn't want your kids to go to the schools in any case.

Policies of new urban populism are being developed and tested on a local level. But those policies will only come to fruition on a national level when they confront inflation, unemployment, the flight of industry out of the city, the need for alternative sources of capital, and other economic issues which are crucial to the survival of the middle class and the protection of poor and working people.

I don't know of any city government anywhere which does not posture being "for the people." But when you watch who makes the decisions and, more importantly, who benefits from those decisions, you begin to understand it's the big money people who have the real clout in the community. But the poet Carl Sandburg once wrote:

> *When I, the People, learn to remember,*
> *When I, the People, use the lessons*
> *Of yesterday and no longer forget who*
> *Robbed me last year, who played me for*
> *A fool—then there will be no speaker*
> *In all the world to say the name:*
> *The People, with any fleck of a sneer*
> *In his voice or any far-off smile*
> *Of derision.*

Adapted from a speech to the National Press Club, 1977.

A Prayer for America

(to be sung as an overture for America)

"My country 'tis of thee. Sweet land of liberty of thee
I sing. . . . From every mountainside, let freedom
ring. . . . Long may our land be bright. With
freedom's holy light. . . ."

"Oh say does that star spangled banner yet wave. O'er
the land of the free and the home of the brave?"

"America, America, God shed grace on thee. And
crown thy good with brotherhood, from sea to shining
sea. . . ."

• • •

I offer these brief remarks today as a prayer for our
country, with love of democracy, and as a celebration
of our country. With love for our country. With hope
for our country. With a belief that the light of freedom

cannot be extinguished as long as it is inside of us. With a belief that freedom rings resoundingly in a democracy each time we speak freely. With the understanding that freedom stirs the human heart and fear stills it. With the belief that a free people cannot walk in fear and faith at the same time.

With the understanding that there is a deeper truth expressed in the unity of the United States. That implicit in the union of our country is the union of all people. That all people are essentially one. That the world is interconnected not only on the material level of economics, trade, communication, and transportation, but innerconnected through human consciousness, through the human heart, through the heart of the world, through the simply expressed impulse and yearning to be and to breathe free.

I offer this prayer for America.

Let us pray that our nation will remember that the unfolding of the promise of democracy in our nation paralleled the striving for civil rights. That is why we must challenge the rationale of the Patriot Act. We must ask, Why should America put aside guarantees of constitutional justice?

How can we justify in effect canceling the First Amendment and the right of free speech, the right to peaceably assemble?

How can we justify in effect canceling the Fourth Amendment, probable cause, the prohibitions against unreasonable search and seizure?

How can we justify in effect canceling the Fifth Amendment, nullifying due process, and allowing for indefinite incarceration without a trial?

How can we justify in effect canceling the Sixth Amendment, the right to prompt and public trial?

How can we justify in effect canceling the Eighth Amendment, which protects against cruel and unusual punishment?

We cannot justify widespread wiretaps and Internet surveillance with judicial supervision, let alone without it.

We cannot justify secret searches without a warrant.

We cannot justify giving the attorney general the ability to designate domestic terror groups.

We cannot justify giving the FBI total access to any type of data which may exist in any system anywhere, such as medical records and financial records.

We cannot justify giving the CIA the ability to target people in this country for intelligence surveillance.

We cannot justify a government which takes from the people our right to privacy and then assumes for its own operations a right to total secrecy.

The attorney general recently covered up a statue of Lady Justice showing her bosom, as if to underscore there is no danger of justice exposing herself at this time, before this administration.

Let us pray that our nation's leaders will not be overcome with fear. Because today there is great fear in our great Capitol. And this must be understood before we can ask about the shortcomings of Congress in the current environment. The great fear began when we had to evacuate the Capitol on September 11. It continued when we had to leave the Capitol again when a bomb scare occurred as members were pressing the CIA during a secret briefing. It continued when we abandoned Washington when anthrax, possibly from a government lab, arrived in the mail.

It continued when the attorney general declared a nationwide terror alert and then the Administration brought the destructive Patriot Bill to the floor of the House.

It continued in the release of the bin Laden tapes at the same time the President was announcing the withdrawal from the Anti-Ballistic Missle (Treaty).

It remains present in the cordoning off of the Capitol. It is present in the camouflaged armed national guardsmen who greet members of Congress each day we enter the Capitol campus. It is present in the labyrinth of concrete barriers through which we must pass each time we go to vote.

The trappings of a state of siege trap us in a state of fear, ill-equipped to deal with the Patriot Games, the Mind Games, the War Games of an unelected president and his undetected vice president.

Let us pray that our country will stop this war. "To provide for the common defense" is one of the formational principles of America.

Our Congress gave the president the ability to respond to the tragedy of September 11. We licensed a response to those who helped bring the terror of September 11. But we the people and our elected representatives must reserve the right to measure the response, to proportion the response, to challenge the response, and to correct the response.

Because we did not authorize the invasion of Iraq.

We did not authorize the invasion of Iran.

We did not authorize the invasion of North Korea.

We did not authorize the bombing of civilians in Afghanistan.

We did not authorize permanent detainees in Guantanamo Bay.

We did not authorize the withdrawal from the Geneva Convention.

We did not authorize military tribunals suspending due process and habeas corpus.

We did not authorize assassination squads.

We did not authorize the resurrection of COINTELPRO.

We did not authorize the repeal of the Bill of Rights.

We did not authorize the revocation of the Constitution.

We did not authorize national identity cards.

We did not authorize the eye of Big Brother to peer from cameras throughout our cities.

We did not authorize an eye for an eye.

Nor did we ask that the blood of innocent people, who perished on September 11, be avenged with the blood of innocent villagers in Afghanistan.

We did not authorize the administration to wage war anytime, anywhere, anyhow it pleases.

We did not authorize war without end.

We did not authorize a permanent war economy.

Yet we are upon the threshold of a permanent war economy. The president has requested a $45.6 billion increase in military spending. All defense-related programs will cost close to $400 billion.

Consider that the Department of Defense has never passed an independent audit. Consider that the Inspector General has notified Congress that the Pentagon cannot properly account for $1.2 trillion in transactions. Consider that in recent years the Department of Defense could not match $22 billion worth of expenditures to the items it purchased, wrote off, as lost, billions of dollars worth of in-transit inventory and stored nearly $30 billion worth of spare parts it did not need.

Yet the defense budget grows with more money for weapons systems to fight a cold war which ended, weapons systems in search of new enemies to create new wars. This has nothing to do with fighting terror.

This has everything to do with fueling a military industrial machine with the treasure of our nation, risking the future of our nation, risking democracy itself with the militarization of thought which follows the militarization of the budget.

Let us pray for our children.

Our children deserve a world without end. Not a war without end. Our children deserve a world free of the terror of hunger, free of the terror of poor health care, free of the terror of homelessness, free of the terror of ignorance, free of the terror of hopelessness, free of the terror of policies which are committed to a world view which is not appropriate for the survival of a free people, not appropriate for the survival of democratic values, not appropriate for the survival of our nation, and not appropriate for the survival of the world.

Let us pray that we have the courage and the will as a people and as a nation to shore ourselves up, to reclaim from the ruins of September 11 our democratic traditions.

Let us declare our love for democracy. Let us declare our intent for peace.

Let us work to make nonviolence an organizing principle in our own society.

Let us recommit ourselves to the slow and painstaking work of statecraft, which sees peace, not war as being inevitable.

Let us work for a world where someday war becomes archaic.

That is the vision which the proposal to create a Department of Peace envisions. Forty-three members of Congress are now cosponsoring the legislation. Let us work for a world where nuclear disarmament is an imperative. That is why we must begin by insisting on the commitments of the ABM treaty. That is why we must be steadfast for nonproliferation.

Let us work for a world where America can lead the day in banning weapons of mass destruction not only from our land and sea and sky but from outer space itself. That is the vision of HR 3616: A universe free of fear. Where we can look up at God's creation in the stars and imagine infinite wisdom, infinite peace, infinite possibilities, not infinite war, because we are taught that the kingdom will come on earth as it is in heaven. Let us pray that we have the courage to replace the images of death which haunt us, the layers of images of September 11, faded into images of patriotism, spliced into images of military mobilization, jump-cut into images of our secular celebrations of the World Series, New Year's Eve, the Superbowl, the Olympics, the strobic flashes which touch our deepest fears, let us replace those images with the work of human relations, reaching out to people, helping our own citizens here at home, lifting the plight of the poor everywhere.

That is the America which has the ability to rally the support of the world.

That is the America which stands not in pursuit of an axis of evil, but which is itself at the axis of hope and faith and peace and freedom. America, America. God shed grace on thee. Crown thy good, America.

Not with weapons of mass destruction. Not with invocations of an axis of evil. Not through breaking international treaties. Not through establishing America as king of a unipolar world. Crown thy good America. America, America. Let us pray for our country. Let us love our country. Let us defend our country not only from the threats without but from the threats within.

Crown thy good, America. Crown thy good with brotherhood, and sisterhood. And crown thy good with compassion and restraint and forbearance and a commitment to peace, to democracy, to economic justice here at home and throughout the world.

Crown thy good, America. Crown thy good, America. Crown thy good.

Speech To the Southern California Americans for Democratic Action, February 17, 2002, Los Angeles, California

A New Horizon for the Democratic Party

I love the West. In some ways, the spirit of my own politics is animated by the mythology of the West: independent, restless, striving, seeking new paths, pushing frontiers, seeking new horizons. Whether contemplating the pioneering spirit atop the Oregon capital in Salem, the daring trek of Lewis and Clark, the California experience of Carey McWilliams, or Seattle's own Space Needle, which flung the dreams of a people toward the stars, the spirit of the West is one of daring, of exploration, of courage and creativity. The narrative of the West has become the narrative of our nation. If all Americans could remember where we came from, we could easily pass through the momentary challenge to our national nerve and recapture the heartfelt rhythms of the land of the free and the home of the brave celebrated in our national anthem.

In November of 1979, I came west to begin my own odyssey. In 1977, I was elected Mayor of Cleveland, on a promise to save Cleveland's 46,000-customer municipally-owned electric system, Muny Light, from a takeover by the privately owned utility, Cleveland Electric Illuminating Company (CEI). Muny Light's rates were as much as 25 percent lower. CEI was in the middle of an aggressive nuclear power building program. A utility monopoly in Cleveland would have enabled CEI to raise utility rates to help pay off their rapidly expanding debt on the nuclear power plants.

How people come to pay for electricity is one of most fascinating economic questions of our time. City-owned utilities, of which there are over two thousand in America, have lower rates, are publicly accountable, and do not have to pay stock dividends and high salaries. CEI tried to block the creation of Muny Light at the turn of the twentieth century. Federal antitrust case records proved CEI tried for years to put Muny Light out of business. CEI damaged Muny's self-sufficiency by blocking repairs to the Muny system through exercising undue influence with the city council.

When Muny looked to purchase power, CEI quietly intervened to stop other utilities from selling to the city. When the city had to turn to CEI for emergency power, CEI charged the city triple what it charged other customers, creating great financial pressures on the public system. It lobbied members of city council to raise Muny's rates to wipe out the price difference. Once, when Muny Light needed emergency power from CEI, the transfer was operated in such a way as to deliberately cause a blackout on the Muny system. CEI used its influence with the media to attack Muny Light as unreliable and worthless, even though the system was making a profit. With military-type precision, the case for a sale of the Muny system soon became the cause of all the radio, television, and newspaper outlets in Cleveland. At the time, Cleveland was the number three corporate headquarters city in America. The corporate community supported the sale. So did both political parties.

The city council and the mayor obliged in 1976 and sold the system for a fraction of its value. I organized a referendum, which blocked the sale. I ran for mayor and won on a promise to save the light system. On December 15, 1978 Ohio's largest bank, Cleveland Trust, demanded that I sell the city's electric system as a precondition for the bank extending $5 million in credit to the city on loans taken out by the previous mayor. Cleveland Trust was CEI's bank, and managed its cash flow. The bank had four interlocking directorates with the utility. It held CEI's pension funds and other investments. With another bank, it was CEI's largest shareholder. If I said yes to the sale, the bank promised not only to renew the city's credit, and gain the cooperation of other banks, but also to grant the city another $50 million in loans. If I said no, Cleveland would become the first American city to go into default on its loans since the Depression.

Where I come from it mattered how much people paid for electricity. I can still remember my mother and father sitting in the kitchen of our apartment, counting pennies on a porcelain-topped table, to make sure they could pay the utility bill. I can still hear those pennies clicking on that porcelain top. So when the bank president demanded sale of our city's electric system, I said no. The city was thrown into default and, a year later, I lost the office it took me ten years to achieve.

After default, I couldn't get a job in Cleveland. I went west, first to California, then Washington State, then Oregon, then New Mexico, then Alaska, seeking a new start, trying to reclaim a career in public life. The years rolled along. I wandered back and forth from the West to Cleveland. Muny Light remained unsold. Fifteen years after default, carried aloft on Muny Light expansion with a system that provided electricity at a savings of up to 30 percent, I began the road back toward national politics with a 1994 election to the Ohio Senate. Two years later I came to congress.

When I was mayor, I was asked to make a conscious choice between competing visions, between whether corporations existed for the city or the city existed for the corporations; between community and commerce; between economic justice and profit; between public and private interest. These are choices which we all make every day in the accommodations we make with our purchases, where we work, where we live, how we travel, and what we eat. Every day, as each one of us chooses, so chooses the world.

A few years ago, I could smell the dynamic tension between the claims of the community and the claims of the free market in the tear gas that invaded the locked-down lobby of this very hotel (Westin, Seattle) during the challenge to the practices of the World Trade Organization. I could feel that tension coursing through the streets of this city when I marched with machinists and moms, with teamsters and turtles in a call for human rights, workers' rights, and environmental quality principles to become integral to our commerce.

The challenge before us today, the challenge before our nation and the world, is whether we accept the beneficence of Lincoln's prayer to create ". . . a government of the people, by the people and for the people," or whether we timidly accept the economic, social, and political consequences of a government of the corporations, by the corporations, and for the corporations.

One hundred years ago, Mayor Tom Johnson of Cleveland set the stage for the establishment of a municipally owned electric company. His credo:

"I believe in the municipal ownership of all public service monopolies, for the same reason that I believe in the municipal ownership of waterworks, of parks, of schools. I believe in the municipal ownership of these monopolies because if you do not own them they will in time own you. They will rule your politics, corrupt your institutions, and finally destroy your liberties."

The implosion of the Enron corporation is a cautionary tale of the danger to the people of our nation, to our economy, and to our political system of the influence of unfettered, unregulated corporations, and the grave risks of privatization. The power industry used its influence at every level of government to create a structure which transferred at least $71 billion from California to itself. It is the Haiku of Hegemony:

Plotting gains. False promise low rates.
Political contributions place.
Regulatory controls erase.
Energy supplies manipulate.
Shortages create.
Blackouts.
Taxpayers bled.
Ratepayers dead.
Windfall profitgate.
Earnings misstate.
Stock inflate.
Enron investigate.
Bailouts by state.
System remains.

This predatory system must be set aside. The only way to ensure that Enron does not happen again is for government at all levels to reclaim *the* role as regulator in the public interest, to restructure electric rates to protect residents and small businesses, to enact windfall profit taxes, and to finance the construction of municipal power systems.

From the darkness that is Enron, I see a new horizon,

where the American community consciously chooses sustainability and ushers in a new era of power—of solar, wind, hydrogen, and other renewable fuels—to provide endless energy upon an endless planet.

The Democratic party must become the party of re-regulation, of public control, of public accountability, of public power—not only in energy, but also in health care.

Through the work of our party, I see a new horizon for health care for all Americans with a universal, single payer system. Today such coverage is available to Americans over the age of sixty-five. We need a new Medicare, Part E (for Everyone), which will relieve the suffering and uncertainty of 44 million Americans who currently have no health coverage and the economic pain of those who are paying exorbitant rates for their health insurance.

Many cannot afford health insurance. Some do not have jobs. Some have lost their jobs. Some people have jobs yet do not have coverage. You and I know people who do not have health coverage, who do not get diagnosed in time. Who end up dying prematurely. This is what happens with a market-based system. Here, again, we are asked to consciously choose our priorities: between the claims of the community and the claims of commerce; Between the requirement for economic justice and the imperative for profit; between the public interest and private interest.

A market-based approach to health care benefits no one except the insurance companies. HMOs are more costly than Medicare. People are getting less care. Fewer people can get a doctor of choice. Fewer people can get the treatment they need. People are waiting longer for appointments. Preexisting illnesses are being used to deny coverage. Physicians are given monetary incentives to deny care.

On January 1, 1999, 400,000 Medicare patients lost their HMO coverage. HMO's claimed the reimbursement rates were too low, so seniors were denied coverage. Remember this date. Because it predicts a trend if we allow Congress to privatize Medicare. We must change this system. Our Democratic Party can claim universal, single-payer health care as our cause; health care for all, in a nation that recognizes that government for the people means all people must have an opportunity to survive.

Today there are senior citizens throughout America who are forced to make cruel choices between paying for prescription drugs and buying food; between prescription drugs and clothing. Seniors are splitting their pills to make prescriptions last, splitting their budgets with six-hundred-dollar monthly prescription bills, splitting their physical and their economic health.

The pharmaceutical industry is the most profitable in America, even more profitable than banking. America is a captive market. Americans pay 64 percent more for the same pharmaceuticals than Canadians. Canadians have a system to control prices. Our government should place limits on the price manufacturers can charge for prescription drugs. We need a new Prescription for America, a regulatory structure which puts a ceiling on drug-company profits the same way credit laws establish what constitutes usury. As with utility rates, our government should lower prices and impose windfall profit taxes to correct excess pricing.

As we look to tomorrow, our government needs to welcome holistic medicine into America's mainstream. Alternative medicine encompasses a focused commitment to personal responsibility for one's health, which is the precursor to a nation of well beings, a nation where people may live qualitatively.

I see an America of retirement security for all. I see a new horizon for Social Security in America, through restoring the age of retirement to sixty-five years, instead of the current sixty-seven years. The normal age for retirement was raised in phases beginning in 1983 from sixty-five to sixty-seven. The reason? People live longer. The economy was transitioning to white collar jobs. But, while people were living longer, they were not working longer, because their bodies wore out. Medical technology has enhanced longevity. Still, increased longevity some-times means people are sicker, longer.

We need to reclaim the benefits of quality life exten-sion for our seniors by reclaiming Social Security benefits at age sixty-five. America can afford it. Social Security's finances are more secure than ever. The fund is solid through the year 2041, without any changes whatsoever. And America is wealthier than at any previous point in Social Security's history.

Yet, advocates of privatization view the Social Security

surplus as a source of revenue to fuel an erratic market. The present Administration has created a commission, which stands for privatization, even in the face of collapsing markets. The proposed privatization of Social Security challenges us once again to consciously choose between community and commerce, between economic justice and profit, between the public and private interest.

As each day's accounting news brings new questions about the true value of a company's stock, about the safety of the individual investor's holding, it becomes an urgent matter of the highest public priority that we not let the retirement security of our nation be lost to profiteers and speculators. It is the obligation of our Democratic Party to keep the historic commitment, which we made to intergenerational security, to economic freedom, and to fairness.

Despite the overwhelming influence which corporations have in the life of our nation, I see a new America of corporate accountability. I see a new horizon in America where ethics, sustainability, and sensible priorities guide corporate conduct in cooperation and harmony with vigilant but fair-minded government regulation.

How do we get there? Our Democratic Party cannot stand by idly while the great economic engines of our society trample workers' rights and human rights, ruin the environment, shatter regulations, sweep aside antitrust laws, destroy competition, accelerate the accumulation of wealth into fewer and fewer hands, and control the government itself. Undue corporate influence has diminished our party, distorted our priorities, eliminated debate, and blurred the line between the political parties.

We need a new relationship between the Democratic Party and corporate America—call it arms-length—so that our party is capable of independently affirming the public interest. We need a new relationship between corporations and our society. Just as our founders understood the need for separation of church and state, we need to institutionalize the separation of corporations and the state. This begins with government taking the responsibility to establish the conditions under which corporations may do business in the United States, including the establishment of a federal corporate charter which describes corporate rights and responsibilities.

Corporations should pay a fair share of taxes. If corporations shift profits offshore to avoid paying taxes, they should not be permitted to operate in the United States. The decrease in corporate tax responsibility is an indication of the rise of corporate power. According to the Institute for Policy Studies, after the 2002 tax cuts, corporations will pay in taxes an amount equivalent to 1.3 percent of the U.S. Gross Domestic Product. In the 1950s they paid taxes of 4.5 percent of the U.S. GDP. Corporations have fewer regulations, pay fewer taxes, and yet have greater influence. (Can there be any clearer indication of the urgency of full public financing of our elections?)

I see an America where the economy works for everyone because everyone is working. I see a new horizon in this country where there is no such thing as an acceptable level of unemployment. Nearly nine million Americans are unemployed. Millions more are not being included in the official count. Average wages are falling. People are taking pay cuts to keep their jobs. The unemployed and the employed alike are experiencing a falling standard of living. The middle class aspirations of many are being dashed.

Where the private sector fails to provide jobs, the public sector has a moral responsibility to do so. People want work, not welfare. And while there ought to be welfare for those unable to work, there ought to be work for those who are able to work and who want to work. And there is enough work to do.

I see a newly rebuilt America. I see a new horizon where America provides a means for massive public works to rebuild our cities, water systems, public transportation systems, schools, parks, and public energy systems. Nearly $150 billion is needed over twenty years to repair and provide for adequate waste-water treatment systems. Another $120 billion is needed for drinking water systems. We need a new financial mechanism to get money to cities and states to begin rebuilding and to put America back to work.

The federal government can give cities and states loans for infrastructure programs to be repaid over a period of thirty years, at zero interest. This would boost economies and spur private investment. A Federal Bank for Infrastructure Maintenance would administer a program of lending $50 billion per year to state and local governments. The money would come from an innovative adaptation of the normal money supply circulation activity of the Federal Reserve Bank. The cost to the American taxpayer is simply the cost of the interest on the loans.

It is up to the Democratic Party to be the advocate of economic progress for all people. We must advance policies which preserve high-wage jobs and support unionization. We should endeavor to condition trade agreements "on the guarantee of internationally recognized rights of workers to organize into independent unions; to prohibit the use of child and forced labor; to be protected by workplace safety laws and to benefit from minimum wage laws."[1] We must take the financial incentive out of capital moving overseas.

I see a Democratic Party that takes a stand for America in the world. I see a new horizon of international relations guided by the progress of the many, not the profits of a few. We must work to reform the International Monetary Fund, the World Bank, and the World Trade Organization. These institutions should not be allowed to condition financial assistance to poor countries by imposing "structural adjustment" policies that deny minimum wages and privatize water, health, retirement, and education systems. If we are prepared to require a higher standard of corporate conduct in the United States, we can require a higher standard of corporate conduct throughout the world through these financial institutions.

1. From a pre-Seattle message from 113 democrats to President Clinton, 1999.

Finally, our party must become the Party of Peace, "to secure the blessings of liberty for ourselves and our posterity." I see a new horizon in America where we work to make nonviolence an organizing principle in our society through the establishment of a cabinet-level Department of Peace. This concept, which is already endorsed by forty-three Democratic members of congress, seeks a new nation which faces the violence in our own society and which fashions a new international policy, which seeks to make war itself archaic. Over one hundred million people, most of them innocent civilians, perished in wars in the twentieth century. Given the destructive power of today's technology, given $400 billion spent annually on the military—given the Administration's statements renewing the nuclear first-strike option, building new nuclear weapons, canceling the ABM Treaty, and putting weapons in space—we must recognize that the survival of humanity depends upon our ability to evolve, to become better than we are, to become more than we are, to protect this fragile world, and to create new worlds of possibility.

In this moment when all is in the balance, it is time for us to rethink the purpose of our party. We must reclaim our historic mission as the party of bold ideas, of national beginnings. We must do so with a passion for democracy and with hearts that are filled with courage and love.

Let us make one more call to action for the generation that suffered the Depression and served in war and is now in its twilight years to remember the dreams of its youth for personal independence.

Let us make in the days ahead one more reveille for our generation, which unfurled its banner of change in the 1960s, believing "we can change the world, rearrange the world. . . ." Let us reclaim the dreams of our own youth for "harmony and understanding, sympathy and trust abounding . . . for the mind's true liberation." And let us have a clarion call for a new generation that longs to hear and to see and to feel real commitment, real conviction, real courage to recreate the future.

Nothing less than the future of our nation and the world is at stake. Americans are waiting for us. The voters are waiting for us. They will show up when we show up. Our greatest power is not political. It is the ability to move the human heart. It is the ability to see our nation as truly indivisible, truly united in the cause of all who long for unity, of all who long for connectivity, of all who seek integrity and wholeness in their own lives, and integrity and wholeness in the life of our nation.

We have done it before. We are the party of FDR and the New Deal. We are the party of JFK and the New Frontier. We are the party of LBJ and the Great Society. We are the party of the realized dream of Martin Luther King. We are the party of the unrealized dreams of Bobby Kennedy. We are the party of Social Security, of Medicare, of civil rights, of equality for women, of a green planet, of a peaceful planet. We are the party of the people.

We stand looking out upon the new horizon of the twenty-first century. It is still daybreak, the sun is about to come up like thunder. And it is our Democratic Party which has the opportunity to widen the bright horizon for all the people, to help people, particularly our youth, to become excited about participating in the process of citizenship, by fearlessly stepping into the crucible of change, by working for new initiatives which will win back people's faith in our government, faith in the political process, faith that their vote matters, and faith in each person's ability to make a difference. One person can make a difference.

Senator Robert Kennedy, addressing students in South Africa who suffered under the yoke of apartheid, understood the potency of the human heart as surmounting all obstacles. He said: "Each time a man (or a woman) stands up for an ideal, acts to improve the lot of others, or strikes out against injustice, he (or she) sends forth a tiny ripple of hope. And crossing each other from a million different centers of energy and daring, those ripples can create a current which can sweep down the mightiest walls of oppression and resistance." This is my commitment. I am sure it is yours, too.

Adapted from a speech to the Democratic National Committee, May 25, 2002, Seattle, Washington.

GLOBAL ACTION TO SUSTAIN PEOPLE

What higher cause or purpose could any of us aspire to than to unite to save the very planet with which billions of people have entrusted us in a special stewardship? Let us not forget that lofty thoughts and words lead us to the starry paths where human destiny transcends our current condition. Our goals must ever be the qualitative transformation of social and political structures.

As Parliamentarians for Global Action we assert our intention and our ability to make a difference in protecting our global environment through concerted action toward sustainability. We have the distinct privilege to think and *act* globally. We have the obligation, as elected officials, to act locally to create energy and other systems in harmony with our neighbors, the environment, and the planet as a whole.

When we speak of sustainability, we speak of support systems that sustain the life of every person living on this planet and of all those who would live on this planet.

Development is often at odds with such systems. In our drive to bring the earth to subjection, humanity has separated itself from nature. This disconnect translates for some as economic progress. In this capacity, nature is brought into subjection at all costs. Air and water quality, principles of biodiversity, indeed humanity itself—all are made subservient to development. Under such conditions a crude transformation is underway.

Our cause is the transformation of the human condition and the triumph of the human spirit: to help our brothers and sisters in their fight for decent living conditions, clean air, clean water, adequate housing, health care, and education. Our cause is human development, which can only succeed when all development is in harmony with the earth and attuned to the natural rhythms that move the tides and ride the currents of fresh air, and pulsate in the human heart, ever striving for freedom and expression. Our challenge is to bring economic systems into harmony with humanity, to create a socially and economically just world, where peace and prosperity abound everywhere.

In doing so we affirm the commonwealth of the world. We affirm support for the purpose of the United Nations and its charter, which enables reciprocity among all countries. We affirm the importance of international treaties, which are the legal basis for global cooperation. We affirm our interdependence and the dignity of each person on this planet. We affirm that all humans have a right to survive and we make the cause of the survival of this world our cause.

In order to fulfill our mission, we must quicken the evolution of our political structures to enable our economic structures to support our democratic structures. An evolutionary governance strengthened through transparency will enable us to make each system within which we work rise to the challenges of our times. Such governance will assist the great business machines of our society in following new thinking, to assure that profit and sustainability exist simultaneously.

For the United States in the twenty-first century, this requires steadfast affirmation of principles of sustainability. It requires recognizing and promoting international cooperation and agreements. It requires affirming, ratifying treaties ranging from the Kyoto Accords to the ABM treaty to the International Criminal Court.

Our mission will require that our country and all nations review and modify all treaties in the service of corporate ethics that do not respect human rights, workers rights, and environmental quality standards. This means reviewing the practices and practical impacts of the General Agreement on Tariffs and Trade, the World Trade Organization, the International Monetary Fund, and the World Bank.

It will require challenging war and global climate change, those twin quandaries which threaten human life and the planet, by ushering in a new era where principles of sustainability and renewal are the basis of every action of each person. To avert war we support existing and new structures for peaceful, nonviolent conflict resolution.

To meet the challenge of global climate change, we

support principles and practical initiatives which point to the path out of the darkness of air too dangerous to breathe and water too dangerous to drink. This includes, of course, principles of accountability for corporations: That they be subject to the rule of national law and to the basic requirements of human rights, workers rights, and environmental quality principles.

Similarly market economics need to be transformed so as to work in harmony with basic human needs for clean air and clean water. Market-based systems which inevitably exclude the poor have no place in the distribution of water. Water is a human right which must stand above market economics and privatization, just as many are learning of the risks of health care and energy left to the market.

The World Conference on Sustainable Development presents each of us with new opportunities to bring practical measures to advance our noble principles. In the United States I will soon announce legislation to create a $50 billion solar venture fund, in cooperation with the United Nations, to introduce solar technologies to developing nations. Parallel legislation will provide incentives for the production and application of solar technologies in the U.S.

As Parliamentarians for Global Action we stand at the threshold of a new world. We understand how profoundly creative is this moment. We know that we have the willingness, the heart, and the spirit to join in the great cause of saving the world.

Let us move forward with great joy, celebrating our brotherhood and sisterhood and the inevitable triumph of truth and justice which occurs whenever people of good will gather together in support of our beautiful planet.

Adapted from a speech to the Parlimentarians for Global Action at the United Nation World Summit on Sustainable Development, August 29, 2002, Johannesburg, South Africa.

ARCHITECTS OF NEW WORLDS

This is the time. This is the place.

This is the place to begin a national movement for renewal, for peace, for reconciliation, and for justice.

Wisconsin, the workshop of political wonders! This is the time and this is the place where we begin to slip from the hold which terror has on our minds and our hearts. On Wisconsin!

Our presence here is the call for a political philosophy which is constructive, transformative, and transcendent. A philosophy based on moral principles and enshrined in law. These self-evident truths of inherent equality of all, the rights of all, and the connection of all are the highest creative forces recognized in our Declaration of Independence, written into our Bill of Rights, and actively present in the soul of every American and freedom-loving person. This is the time today, to reconnect with the highest purposes of our nation.

This was a gift. This was the gift of our founders: a new

nation with the ability to adapt to the future of our dreams. Now is the time to restore that gift through traveling with faith and with courage, to follow the upward spiral path to the unseen heights of human endeavor; to create an evolutionary politics of creativity, of vision, of heart, of compassion, of joy; to create a new nation and a new world using the power of love, of community, of participation; to transform our politics, and yes, to transform ourselves.

As we begin, let us recall the power of a dream. "We are such stuff as dreams are made on," wrote Shakespeare in *The Tempest*. Let us recall the dreamers, the architects of new worlds, as we reflect on the power of our plans to bring architecture and substance to our dreams.

The dreamers:

—The dream of peace and personal transcendence, in the life of Christ.

—The dream of racial equality, the life of Dr. King.

—The dream of union through equality, the life of Lincoln.

—The dream of gender equality, Susan B. Anthony.

—The dream of freedom through soul force, Gandhi.

—Nationhood, Washington.

—Democracy, Jefferson.

—Compassion, Mother Teresa.

—Environmental justice, Rachel Carson.

—Justice for workers, John L. Lewis.

—Corporate accountability, Ralph Nader.

—Progressive economics, Bob LaFollette.

Let us today seek to find that place within each of us where dreams are made, where our highest aspirations take shape. Let us confirm the power of our humanity by giving architecture and substance to the dreams we have for our nation, so that the promised land of social and economic justice that is within our dreams will soon be within our sight.

We seek a newer nation, in the spirit of Bob LaFollette, who said "America is not made, it's in the making." And when he said that, years ago in 1924, as an independent progressive candidate for president, you and I know there was one major city that he carried in this nation. One major city that matched this major state, and that city was Cleveland, Ohio. So it's good to be here today, reconnecting with that progressive position, which is where we all ought to be in this nation. Wisconsin shows the way; Cleveland replies.

Let us remake America by reconnecting with a higher purpose to bring peace within and without, to come into harmony with nature, to confirm and to secure the basic rights of our brothers and sisters.

Ours is a worthy purpose which can be addressed through addressing the practical aspirations of all people for economic opportunity, for peace, for jobs, for a living wage, for education, for housing, for health care, for clean air and clean water, and for retirement security.

Let us remake America through calling for the establishment of a Department of Peace. It is time to make nonviolence an organizing principle in our society, for domestic as well as international policy.

The only weapon that can save the world is nonviolence, said Gandhi. We can begin this practice today, not only here in Wisconsin as you do, but all over this country, by calling upon the administration in Washington to stop the talk of war, stop the planning for war, stop the bombing, and stop plans for an invasion of Iraq!

The American people do not want war on Iraq!

The American people want peace.

They do not want war on Iraq!

Iraq did not cause 9/11. Iraq is not connected with Al Qaeda. Iraq had no connection to the anthrax attacks on our nation. There's no evidence Iraq has weapons of mass destruction, or the ability to deliver such weapons if it had them, or the intention to do so. There is no reason for war against Iraq. Stop the drumbeat. Stop the war talk. Pull back from the abyss of unilateral action and preemptive strikes.

It is time, instead, to explore more peaceful, consistent rhythms of the language of peace, of cooperation, mutuality, of recognition that all people—all people—have a right to life, liberty, and pursuit of happiness.

America should reach out to the global community to establish global security, work with the nations of the world, work with the United Nations. We should use our allies—allies like Russia which just concluded a forty billion-dollar trade agreement with Iraq—to begin anew honest negotiations for honest weapons inspection.

The time has come for us to end the sanctions against Iraq, because those sanctions punish the people of Iraq because they have Saddam Hussein as their leader. We should end the sanctions against Iraq which have been instrumental in causing the deaths of hundreds of thousands of children. We should also drop the self-defeating policy of regime change.

Policies of aggression and assassination are not worthy of any nation with a democratic tradition, let alone a nation of people who love liberty and whose sons and daughters sacrifice to maintain that democracy.

The question isn't whether or not America has the military power for victory. The question is not whether America has the ability to destroy Saddam Hussein and Iraq. The question is whether we destroy something essential in this nation, by asserting that America has the right to do so anytime we well please.

America cannot and should not be the world's policeman. America cannot and should not try to pick the leaders of other nations. Nor should America and the American people be pressed into the service of international oil interests and arms dealers.

We must work to bring Iraq back into the community of nations, not through destruction, but through constructive action worldwide. America, with the international community, can help negotiate a resolution with Iraq which encompasses unfettered inspections, the end of sanctions, and the cessation of the regime-change policy. America can do this. We have the power to do this. We must have the will to do this. It must be the will of the American people expressed through the direct action of peaceful insistence, and this is the place to begin that. If we begin this in any place in America, begin it here!

We must change the metaphor of our society from one of war to peace. The Department of Defense now requires in excess of $400 billion for its activities. A Department of Peace can be an effective counterbalance, redirecting our national energies towards nonviolent intervention, mediation, and conflict resolution on all matters of human security.

A Department of Peace can look at the domestic issues which our society faces and often ignores as we focus on matters international, because we have a problem with violence in our own society, and we need to look at it and address it in a structured way. And so a Department of Peace on a domestic level would look at issues of domestic violence, spousal abuse, violence in our schools, police-community relations, racial violence, violence against gays—that entire social pathology which is reflected in a nation which doesn't live up to its potential.

And yet we know, Americans have proven over and over again we're a nation that can rise to the challenges of our times, because our people have that capacity. And so, the concept of a Department of Peace is the vehicle by which we express our belief that we have the capacity to evolve as a people, that someday we could look back at this moment and understand that we took the steps along the way to make war archaic. War is not inevitable. Peace is inevitable!

This is our birthright as citizens of a common planet. This is our birthright as citizens of a democratic society.

Today, America's attention is riveted on whether or not we're going to war. America's attentions would be much better placed if we found a way to bring universal health care into our society; if we found a way to guarantee that every young person in every state in our union could have free college education because we can afford it; If we found a way to wipe out unemployment, and bring a new WPA program, so everyone could have a job, so we could rebuild our cities. America has work to do.

In my district, senior citizens tell me about the high cost of prescription drugs. Drug companies are marking up those prescription drugs ten and twenty times. People are splitting their pills in order to try to make prescriptions last. They're forgoing meals in order to make their prescriptions last.

We need an America that is humane enough to recognize the basic needs of our own people. We have the ability and we certainly have the resources to do it. We must have the will. America has much work to do.

We have much work to do as a nation among nations. America should be leading the way in international cooperation.

I just came back from Johannesburg, South Africa, where I was at the World Summit on Sustainable Development. I will tell you that nations around the world are waiting for America to participate in world efforts to deal with the challenge of global climate change. It's time that we did!

It's time that we ratified the Kyoto Agreement!

It's time that we worked toward global reductions in nuclear arms!

It's time that we got rid of nuclear weapons!

It's time that we ended once and for all nuclear testing!

It's time that we begin to have an International Criminal Court, a biological weapons convention, a chemical weapons convention, and to recognize in all areas that international cooperation is the path to the future. International cooperation is the path of peace. International cooperation is the path that all Americans want to take. We have to insist our leaders take us in that direction.

It's time for peace. It's time for cooperation.

It's time for recognition of our interdependence. It's time for realizing the human family as one. What affects any one of us affects all of us. Our brothers and sisters in some faraway lands rely on us for attention, for conscious application of our hearts and our concerns about their rights. They rely on us for food. They do not rely on us for bombs. We should not be sending them bombs!

Today, in Wisconsin, here in Baraboo, you have the opportunity to restart the American evolution. To cause our country to evolve into a country which truly cares about the economic progress of all people.

Which is truly invested in the unfolding of the higher cause of each person's life.

Which recognizes its responsibility to regulate capital markets.

Which recognizes its responsibility to stop the further widening of gaps in wealth in this country.

Which recognizes its responsibility to make for more equitable distribution of the wealth in our society.

Which recognizes its responsibility to make sure that this doesn't become a society where the rich get richer, and the poor get poorer, and the middle class disappears.

We're at an important moment in this country's history. It's a moment when we cannot afford to be on the sidelines. We have to be involved, with our heads and with our hearts, and with a passionate belief in the destiny of our country and the destiny we still have to fulfill in realizing the dream of democracy. Of not simply political democracy, but of economic democracy—because you cannot have a political democracy until you have an economic democracy.

So our efforts must be for corporate accountability, for making sure corporations pay a fair share of the taxes; to make sure that people who work for a corporation have their pensions protected.

Our efforts have to be directed at the functions of those engines of international corporate capitalism: those organizations embodied in the World Trade Organization and the IMF. We must make sure that we take a strong stand on behalf of workers' rights, human rights, and environmental quality principles in all of our trade agreements. It's essential.

It's time that we reclaim the power of the American people and begin the federal chartering of corporations.

And it's time we begin to reclaim our government. Senator Feingold made a valiant effort and needs to be applauded and congratulated. What we need in this country, once and for all, is public financing of elections. Take the corporations out of it!

Yesterday I joined with members of Congress in New York City in a special commemoration. For the second time in more than two hundred years we met in New York City in Federal Hall. We were there in solidarity with the people of New York and all those people everywhere who lost loved ones on 9/11.

And as we sat there in federal hall, as the "Star Spangled Banner" was being sung, I thought of those words of Francis Scott Key, who wrote "Oh say, does that Star-Spangled Banner yet wave / O'er the land of the free and the home of the brave?"

In his writing, he connected, plaintively, freedom and bravery. Every time Americans sing this, we need to remember: To remain the land of the free, it will take courage.

It will take courage to stand up.

It will take courage to speak out.

It will take courage to challenge a government that goes the wrong way.

It will take courage in order to save our democracy.

It will take courage in order to save a benevolent role for America in the world.

Oh say, does that Star Spangled Banner yet wave / O'er the land of the free and the home of the brave?

Does it? Does it? Does it?

We begin today to renew this country, to bring this

country back toward an upward path. The future of humanity can be secure, because we stand for democratic values. Because we stand for peace and because we stand for social and economic justice. Because we care enough to challenge our government in a moment of crisis to set our government back on the right path.

God bless you and Wisconsin for all that you have done in renewing a long tradition for progressive politics to ensure that the conscience of America remains alert to the challenges of the present day and the challenges of the future.

God bless America, and God bless Wisconsin.

Thank you very much.

From an extemporaneous speech (edited) given by Representative Dennis Kucinich on September 7, 2002 in Baraboo, Wisconsin. Kucinich was the keynote speaker at the "Fighting Bob Fest."

A Second Renaissance

Last week I joined hundreds of members of Congress in solemn commemoration of 9/11 and in solidarity with New Yorkers at federal hall in the city. You can sense a special energy at this sacred shrine to democracy where George Washington was sworn in, where a Congress of two centuries ago received the Bill of Rights. As I stood there in a moment of reflection, I could envision that congress of long ago gathering as a galaxy of stars cascaded from the sky through the circular opening above the rotunda.

In my mind's eye, I could see a galaxy of stars representing universal principles pouring into the venerable site, informing the pledge Washington made to a new nation, freedom's holy light illuminating the Bill of Rights. In that moment I had a new understanding that this flag, as spangled with stars as a bolt of heaven itself, connects the United States with eternal principles of unity, of brotherhood, of sisterhood.

The energy of the stars present at the birth of this nation is with us still. It is upon that dark blue cloth of our flag. One bright star shines for hope. Another star for optimism. Another for well-being. One for freedom. One for abundance. One for creativity. One for togetherness. One for peace. One star to wish upon to create your highest aspirations, to make your dreams come true.

This, our country and our very selves are all made of stars, as a popular song goes. This is who we are. This is what gives higher meaning to being an American. This is what gives higher meaning to patriotism. I love our flag. Though some would make it stand for chaos and war, I see the field of stars as standing for the highest expression of human unity.

A higher meaning of the United States is that we express wholeness through the unity of fifty states. "Out of many we are one." We present ourselves to the world as an exemplification of the principle of oneness, of the universality of all, of the confirmation of one in the many. The World: "Out of many nations we are one." Universality! This is where we come from.

The idea of America emerged from the intellectual energy, the heart energy and the spirit energy of the Renaissance. The genesis in a journey of "lovers marrying their fortunes together," bound for America, looking for that lamp lifted beside the golden door of liberty.

The quest for universal principles of justice, of human rights, of civil rights, of opportunity, of a meaningful future is what caused millions to see America as the light of nations. These universal principles are stars by which those who came to our shores sailed. These are stars which can guide us past the shoals of arms dealers and oil interests who today would crash our ship of state upon the rocks of war.

America has a higher destiny. As with generations past, our destiny can takes us to places we have never been, or can only imagine. Places of peace. Places of plenty. Places of hope. Places of love. We have a right to live our ideals. That is our birthright. We should not trade it for the pretensions of empire. Nor for delusions of grandeur, nor for all the gold in Fort Knox, all the tea in China, or all the oil in Iraq. America has a higher destiny.

Today I want to speak to you about the America that can be. About reestablishing the context of our nation. About remythologizing America. About *A Second Renaissance* which can begin in this nation, with this generation.

First let us travel to the place where civilization was born thousands of years ago, upon the banks of the Tigris and the Euphrates. Let us see if there, instead of dancing with death, and killing untold thousands of innocent people, we can change directions, pull back from war with Iraq, change the outcome, connect with our aspirations for peace, and reclaim our ingenuity and creativity in human relations.

Why is war with Iraq presented as inevitable? Isn't it time to insist that our leaders suspend their incessant talk of preventive war, of assumed right to unilateral action? Isn't it time for insistence upon preventive diplomacy and our obligations to work with the world community on matters of global security?

Why is this war presented as inevitable? The headlines from the *New York Times* of September 12, 2002 read:

Bush to Warn UN: Act on Iraq or US Will;
He Leads Nation in Mourning at Terror Sites

There is no credible evidence linking Iraq with 9/11, with Al Qaeda, or with the anthrax attacks. There is no credible evidence that Iraq has usable weapons of mass destruction, the ability to deliver those weapons, or the intention to do so. Though Iraq possessed and used such weapons years ago, they did so, quite sad to say, with the knowledge of, and sometimes with materials from, the United States.

During the Administration of Ronald Reagan, sixty helicopters were sold to Iraq. Later reports said Iraq used U.S. helicopters to spray Kurds with chemical weapons. According to the *Washington Post,* Iraq used mustard gas against Iran with the help of intelligence from the CIA. Intelligence reports cited the use of nerve gas by Iraq against Iran. Iraq's punishment? The U.S. reestablished full diplomatic ties around Thanksgiving of 1984.

Throughout 1989 and 1990, U.S. companies, with the permission of the first Bush government, sent to the government of Saddam Hussein tons of mustard gas precursors, live cultures for bacteriological research, helped to build a chemical weapons factory, supplied West Nile virus, supplied fuel air explosive technology, computers for weapons technology, hydrogen cyanide precursors, computers for weapons research and development, and vacuum pumps and bellows for nuclear weapons plants. "We have met the enemy," said Walt Kelly's Pogo, "and he is us." *Us*.

By the way, it's called the Department of Defense, not the Department of Offense. Unilateral action on the part of the United States, or in partnership with Great Britain, would for the first time set our nation on the bloodstained path of aggressive war, a sacrilege upon the memory of those who fought to defend this country. America's moral authority would be undermined throughout the world. It would signal for Russia to invade Georgia; China, Taiwan; North Korea, the South; India, Pakistan; and it would destabilize the entire gulf and middle east region.

There is a way out.

We need a comprehensive solution to the crisis in Iraq.

It must involve the United Nations and can be facilitated by Russia which just signed a $40 billion trade agreement with Iraq.

Inspections for weapons of mass destruction should begin immediately.

Inspectors must have free and unfettered access to all sites.

New negotiations must begin concerning the counterproductive policies of regime change and sanctions.

Emergency relief should be expedited.

Free trade, except in arms, must be permitted.

Foreign investments must be allowed.

The assets of Iraq abroad must be restored.

A regional zone free of weapons of mass destruction should be established.

If we can take a new direction in Iraq and the region we can begin a new era of peace. We can refocus our efforts on the conflict between the Palestinians and the Israelis. We can bring new initiatives to help Pakistan and India resolve Kashmir.

The United States can repair its position in the world community, through cooperation, not confrontation. We can change the world for the better.

We can look to heaven itself for guidance. We can begin by banning any research, planning, or deployment of weapons in outer space. Human destiny has always been linked with the stars. How grim that America is planning to put weapons in outerspace, to seize the ultimate high ground, to attempt to gain strategic advantage over every nation on earth. We must turn back from such arrogance. We must let the name of peace be hallowed on earth as it is in the heavens with a Space Preservation Treaty. We must direct our efforts toward solving conflicts on this planet rather than spreading war in perpetuity, throughout the universe, in a plan paradoxically called "Vision 2020."

I have a vision of nations working together, cooperatively, using what President Franklin Delano Roosevelt called the "science of human relationships." That is the basis for the creation of a Department of Peace, which seeks to make nonviolence an organizing principle in our society for domestic as well as international policy. War is not inevitable unless we refuse to work for peace, patiently and tirelessly.

I envision a new U.S. leadership to end the threat of nuclear destruction by realizing the promise of the Nonproliferation Treaty. Sixteen nations possess, are pursuing, or are capable of acquiring nuclear weapons. Now is the time to provide incentives to stop the nuclear arms race, to stop building nuclear weapons, and to stop testing. America should restore the ABM treaty and begin again with Russia toward true arms reductions, toward the day when all nuclear weapons are abolished.

America can lead those twenty-six nations which possess, pursue, or are trying to acquire chemical weapons of mass destruction to move toward participation in the Chemical Weapons convention and agree to have such weapons eliminated worldwide.

America can lead the way toward the destruction of all biological weapons of mass destruction by signing on to the Biological Weapons Convention. Twenty nations have designs on such weapons. Let America lead the way toward abolishing biological weapons.

We have much work to do to regain world leadership in ending the proliferation of Small Arms by signing the Small Arms Treaty and to eliminate the scourge of land mines.

America can help to strengthen the cause of international justice by agreeing to the International Criminal

Court. Certainly a nation which has an interest in bringing to justice those in violation of international law should support an international court which would accomplish just that.

Two weeks ago I represented the United States at the World Summit on Sustainable Development. There, Congressman George Miller of California, Earl Blumenauer of Oregon, and I called for our nation to join with the world community in solving the challenge of global climate change, and work to reduce carbon emissions and greenhouse gases. America must lead the way toward sustainability and renewable energies. As the first step, I joined with Mayor Jerry Brown proposing a $50 billion solar initiative in cooperation with Mikhail Gorbachev's Global Green.

It is the United States which can lead the way toward a global community which is inclusive and sustainable, which promotes democratic values, and which enables the growth of the potential and the health of each person by putting human rights, workers rights, and environmental quality principles into each and every trade agreement.

There is much to do on the world stage. But we cannot do it by creating war when we ought to be working for peace. Iraq is not an imminent threat. But an unemployment rate which approaches 6 percent is an imminent threat. Forty-one million Americans without health insurance is an imminent threat. The high cost of prescription drugs, an imminent threat. Unregulated energy companies which charge confiscatory rates for electricity and gas are an imminent threat. Large corporations which lie about their value and deprive stockholders of their life savings constitute an imminent threat. Seniors losing their pensions. That's an imminent threat.

So too is the climate of fear which is being cycled in this country. Each time a civil liberty is rolled back or undermined in America, a little bit of our free nation dies. Each government report which drums terror and fear weakens our nation. When Francis Scott Key wrote "Oh say, does that Star Spangled Banner yet wave / O'er the land of the free and the home of the brave?" he made the essential connection between democracy and courage.

Courage will guide our nation through this crisis. Courage will enable us to set our government right. Courage will enable us to go to the campuses, to labor halls, to church halls, and to the streets to organize against a war which will undermine our nation, ruin our reputation, kill innocent people, and damage the economy of our nation and the world.

We are at a critical and creative moment in human history where we have it within our power to change the world. It is about evolutionary politics which follows an evolutionary consciousness. We can do it by changing the way we look at the world. By contemplating and realizing the universal brotherhood and sisterhood of all persons. We can do it by tapping our own unlimited potential to think anew. Imagine if we could look at our nation with the same daring with which our founders gazed.

Imagine if we could regain the capacity of spirit which animated freedom of speech, the right to assemble, the right to vote, freedom from fear, freedom from want.

I tell you there is another America out there. It is ready to be called forward. It is the America of our dreams. It is the America of the flag full of stars. It is the America which is in our hearts and we can make it the heart of the world. Thank you.

Speech to the Redwood Sequoia Congress, University of California, September 14, 2002, Berkeley California.

Spirit and Stardust

As one studies the images of the Eagle Nebula, brought back by the Hubble telescope from that place in deep space where stars are born, one can imagine the interplay of cosmic forces across space and time, of matter and spirit dancing to the music of the spheres atop an infinite sea of numbers.

Spirit merges with matter to sanctify the universe. Matter transcends, to return to spirit. The interchangeability of matter and spirit means the starlit magic of the outermost life of our universe becomes the soul-light magic of the innermost life of our self. The energy of the stars becomes us. We become the energy of the stars. Stardust and spirit unite and we begin: one with the universe; whole and holy; from one source, endless creative energy, bursting forth, kinetic, elemental; we—the earth, air, water, and fire-source of nearly fifteen billion years of cosmic spiraling.

We begin as a perfect union of matter and spirit. We

receive the blessings of the Eternal from sky and earth. In our outstretched hands, we can feel the energy of the universe. We receive the blessings of the Eternal from water, which nourishes and sanctifies life. We receive the blessings of the Eternal from the primal fire, the pulsating heart of creation. We experience the wonder of life, multidimensional and transcendent. We extend our hands upward, and we are showered with abundance. We ask and we receive. A universe of plenty flows to us, through us. It is in us. We become filled with endless possibilities.

We need to remember where we came from; to know that we are one; to understand that we are of an undivided whole: race, color, nationality, creed, and gender are beams of light, refracted through one great prism. We begin as perfect and journey through life to become more perfect in the singularity of "I" and in the multiplicity of "we"; a more perfect union of matter and spirit. This is human striving. This is where, in Shelley's words, ". . . hope creates from its own wreck the thing it contemplates." This is what Browning spoke of: Our "reach exceeding [our] grasp." This is a search for heaven within, a quest for our eternal home.

In our soul's Magnificat, we become conscious of the cosmos within us. We hear the music of peace, we hear the music of cooperation, we hear the music of love. We hear harmony, a celestial symphony. In our soul's forgetting, we become unconscious of our cosmic birthright, plighted with disharmony, disunity, torn asunder from the stars in a disaster well-described by Matthew Arnold in

"Dover Beach": ". . . the world, which seems to lie before us like a land of dreams, so various, so beautiful, so new, hath really neither joy, nor love, nor light, nor certitude, nor peace, nor help for pain. And we are here, as on a darkling plain, swept with confused alarms of struggle and flight, where ignorant armies clash by night." Today Dover Beach is upon the shores of the Potomac River in Washington, D.C. Our leaders think the unthinkable and speak of the unspeakable inevitability of nuclear war; of a nuclear attack on New York City, of terrorist attacks throughout our nation; of war against Iraq using nuclear weapons; of biological and chemical weapon attacks on civilian populations; of catastrophic global climate change; of war in outer space.

When death (not life) becomes inevitable, we are presented with an opportunity for great clarity, for a great awakening, to rescue the human spirit from the arms of Morpheus through love, through compassion, and through integrating spiritual vision and active citizenship to restore peace to our world. The moment that one world is about to end, a new world is about to begin. We need to remember where we came from. Because the path home is also the way to the future.

In the city I represent in the United States Congress, there is a memorial to peace, named by its sculptor, Marshall A. Fredericks, the "Fountain of Eternal Life." A figure rises from the flames, his gaze fixed to the stars, his hands positioned sextant-like, as if measuring the distance. Though flames of war from the millions of hearts and the dozens of places wherein it rages may lick at our consciousness, our gaze must be fixed upward to invoke universal principles of unity, of cooperation, of compassion; to infuse our world with peace; to ask for the active presence of peace; to expand our capacity to receive it; and to express it in our everyday life. We must do this fearlessly and courageously and not breathe in the poison gas of terror. As we receive, so shall we give.

As citizen-diplomats of the world, we send peace as conscious expression wherever, whenever, and to whomever it is needed: to the Middle East, to the Israelis and the Palestinians, to the Pakistanis and the Indians, to Americans and Al Qaeda, to the people of Iraq, and to all those locked in deadly combat. And we fly to be with the bereft, with those on the brink, to listen compassionately, setting aside judgment and malice to become peacemakers, to intervene, to mediate, to bring ourselves back from the abyss, to bind up the world's wounds.

As we aspire to universal brotherhood and sisterhood, we harken to the cry from the heart of the world and respond affirmatively to address through thought, word, and deed conditions which give rise to conflict: economic exploitation, empire building, political oppression, religious intolerance, poverty, disease, famine, homelessness, struggles over control of water, land, minerals, and oil.

We realize that what affects anyone, anywhere affects everyone, everywhere. As we help others to heal, we heal ourselves. Our vision of interconnectedness resonates with new networks of world citizens in nongovernmental organizations linking from numberless centers of energy, expressing the emergence of a new, organic whole, seeking unity within and across national lines. New transnational Web-based e-mail and telecommunications systems transcend governments and carry within them the power of qualitative transformation of social and political structures and a new sense of creative intelligence. If governments and their leaders, bound by hierarchy and patriarchy, wedded to military might for legitimacy, fail to grasp the implications of an emerging world consciousness for cooperation, for peace, and for sustainability, they may become irrelevant.

As citizen-activists the world over merge, they can become an irresistible force to create peace and protect the planet. From here will come a new movement to abolish nuclear weapons and all weapons of mass destruction. From here will come the demand for sustainable communities, for new systems of energy, transportation, and commerce. From here comes the future rushing in on us.

How does one acquire the capacity for active citizenship? The opportunities exist every day. In Cleveland, citizens have developed the ability to intercede when schools are scheduled to be closed, and have kept the schools open; to rally to keep hospitals open; to save industries which provide jobs; to protect neighborhood libraries from curtailment of service; to improve community policing; to meet racial, ethnic, and religious intolerance openly and directly. Active citizenship begins with an envisioning of the desired outcome and a conscious application of spiritual principles. I know. I have worked with the people in my own community. I have seen the dynamic of faith in self, faith in one's ability to change things, faith in one's ability to prevail against the odds through an appeal to the spirit of the world for help, through an appeal to the spirit of community for participation, through an appeal to the spirit of cooperation, which multiplies energy. I have seen citizens challenge conditions without condemning anyone, while invoking principles of non-opposition and inclusion of those who disagree.

I have seen groups of people overcome incredible odds as they become aware they are participating in a cause beyond self, and sense the movement of the inexorable which comes from unity. When you feel this principle at work, when you see spiritual principles form the basis of active citizenship, you are reminded once again of the merging of stardust and spirit. There is creativity. There is magic. There is alchemy.

Citizens across the United States are now uniting in a great cause to establish a Department of Peace, seeking nothing less than the transformation of our society, to make nonviolence an organizing principle, to make war archaic through creating a paradigm shift in our culture for human development, for economic and political justice, and for violence control. Its work in violence control will be to support disarmament, treaties, peaceful coexistence, and peaceful consensus-building. Its focus on economic and political justice will examine and enhance resource distribution and human and economic rights, and strengthen democratic values.

Domestically, the Department of Peace would address violence in the home, spousal abuse, child abuse, gangs, and police-community relations conflicts, and work with individuals and groups to achieve changes in attitudes that examine the mythologies of cherished world views, such as "violence is inevitable" or "war is inevitable." Thus it will help with the discovery of new selves and new paths toward peaceful consensus.

The Department of Peace will also address human development and the unique concerns of women and children. It will envision and seek to implement plans for peace education, not simply as a course of study, but as a template for all pursuits of knowledge within formal educational settings.

Violence is not inevitable. War is not inevitable. Nonviolence and peace are inevitable. We can make of this world a gift of peace which will confirm the presence of universal spirit in our lives. We can send into the future the gift which will protect our children from fear, from harm, from destruction.

Carved inside the pediment which sits atop the marble columns at the entrance to the United States House of Representatives is a sentinel. Standing resolutely inside this "Apotheosis of Democracy" is a woman, a shield by her left side, with her outstretched right arm protecting a child sitting happily at her feet.

The child holds the lamp of knowledge under the protection of this patroness.

This wondrous sculpture by Paul Wayland Bartlett is entitled "Peace Protecting Genius." Not with nuclear arms, but with a loving maternal arm is the knowing child Genius shielded from harm. This is the promise of hope over fear. This is the promise of love which overcomes all. This is the promise of faith which overcomes doubt. This is the promise of light which overcomes darkness. This is the promise of peace which overcomes war.

Thank you.

Praxis Peace Institute Conference, Dubrovnik, Croatia, Sunday, June 9, 2002.

ON WAR
AND
PEACE

Peace As a Civil Right

"Oh hear my song, thou God of all the nations, a song of peace for their land and for mine."

—Jean Sibelius, *This Is My Song, Finlandia*

The life of Dr. Martin Luther King shines like the sun through the clouds which hover over this nation, casting a beam of light whenever darkness seeks to envelope us, illuminating our way over the rocky, perilous ground until we can envision the upward path toward social and economic justice.

This evening we reflect on his challenge to America's prosecution of a war in Vietnam as we ponder an America poised to once again use its destructive power against a nation of people already broken by war, by U.S. sanctions, by an uncaring leader. America stands ready to accelerate the bombing over major cities in Iraq, to destroy lives, families, houses, buildings, water systems, electric systems, to light fires to force populations to move, to engage in house-to-house combat. All in the name of fighting terrorism. In the name of removing weapons of mass destruction.

In his speech thirty-five years ago at Riverside Church

in New York City, Dr. King created the synthesis of peace and civil rights. "Somehow this madness must cease," Dr. King said then of the annihilation of the Vietnamese people and their nation. "I speak as a child of God and brother to the suffering poor of Vietnam. I speak for those whose land is being laid waste, whose homes are being destroyed, whose culture is being subverted."

Let us contemplate his words. "Somehow this madness must cease." Tonight we call for an end to the pretext for war. Tonight we call for the end of justification for war. Tonight we call for the end of a military buildup toward war. Tonight we call for the end of war in the hearts of those who desire war. Tonight we call for the beginning of compassion. Tonight we call for human dignity. Tonight we call for human unity.

"I speak for the poor of America who are paying the double price of smashed hopes at home, and death and corruption in Vietnam," Dr. King said.

Once again the hopes of people of two nations are being smashed by weapons in the name of eliminating weapons. Let us abolish weapons of mass destruction at home. Joblessness is a weapon of mass destruction. Poverty is a weapon of mass destruction. Hunger is a weapon of mass destruction. Homelessness is a weapon of mass destruction. Poor health care is a weapon of mass destruction. Poor education is a weapon of mass destruction. Discrimination is a weapon of mass destruction.

Let us abolish such weapons of mass destruction here at home. Let us use hundreds of billions of our tax dollars, which some would cast upon Iraq in bombs and warring troops, instead for the restoration of the American Dream, to rebuild our economy and to expand opportunities for all. We have a duty to assert our human needs as a people and not to yield them for the base concerns of an unresponsive government: We have a right to a job. We have a right to decent housing. We have a right to health care. We have a right to food fit to eat, air fit to breathe, and water fit to drink. Peace is a civil right which makes other human rights possible. Peace is the precondition for our existence. Peace permits our continued existence.

"I speak as a citizen of the world," Dr. King said, "for the world, as it stands aghast at the path we have taken. I speak as one who loves America, to the leaders of our nation: The great initiative in this war is ours, the initiative to stop it must be ours."

Today the world is watching, once again, aghast at an America resolutely poised for war. The UN is already predicting a war against Iraq will bring about at least five hundred thousand casualties among the men, women, and children of Iraq who are not foreigners, but are our brothers and sisters.

It is up to us to rally our countrymen and countrywomen to the cause of peace, for the sake of peace, and for the sake of the innocents and whatever innocence of our own we may rescue. For the sake of truth, too.

No justification whatsoever exists for the United States, the United Nations, or any institution whose existence celebrates justice or human unity to wage war against Iraq.

On September 12, 2001, a little more than twenty-four hours after the planes hit the World Trade Center, the Secretary of Defense, in a meeting at the White House, called for immediate strikes against Iraq. Bob Woodward reports in his book *Bush at War*: "Rumsfeld was raising the possibility that they could take advantage of the opportunity offered by the terrorist attacks to go after Saddam immediately."

In sixteen months since America was attacked, no credible evidence has been presented that Iraq perpetrated 9/11, or conspired in 9/11. Iraq was not responsible for the anthrax attack on our country. Nor does Iraq have missile strike capability against the U.S., usable weapons of mass destruction, nor the intention to use them against us.

It is more than strange that while no credible connection has been made between Iraq and 9/11, that the Administration blocked efforts at an early official inquiry into 9/11, while beating the drums to attack Iraq.

Why is the Administration targeting Iraq? Oil. America has become increasingly reliant on imported oil. The future of an oil-dominated economy rests in the Gulf region. Instead of a new energy policy, we get a new war of "good" acting against "evil."

To be sure, the dictator Saddam Hussein is an easy target, for murder of his own people. He was an easy target, too, years ago when supported by the United States, notwithstanding his cruelty.

When war is already in the hearts of those who lead this nation, because our leaders aspire to dominate oil markets, or expand arms trade, or desire world empire, or to distract from failures domestically, what are the American people to do? Do we just sit and watch while the United States moves next to declare war against North Korea, or Iran?

In the spirit of Dr. King, we must reject this White House war mentality and the unfortunate energy policy which spawns it, or we are facing endless war over diminishing resources. The Administration has made its intentions for war known. Now the American people must make our intentions known for peace.

We must reject war with Iraq. We must insist that the UN inspection process continue. As long as the UN inspection presence is at work in Iraq there is the possibility that Iraq can be disarmed, rebuilt, and reintegrated into the community of nations.

Yet predictions of war swirling around the Capitol involve not if, but when, and whether America "goes it alone." The question is not whether we shall go to war with the UN or without the UN The question is why should we go to war at all? Some have made a cause of twelve empty "war heads" recently discovered. There is something lacking in the war heads as there is something lacking in the heads of those who want war.

The narrow-minded drive for regime change will have severe consequences. Regime change means war. Regime change means invasion. It means occupation. It means colonization. It means the death of countless

Iraqi citizens and the deaths of countless American servicemen and servicewomen. And the waste of up to $1.9 trillion in our tax dollars, wrecking our economy while, at the same time, the Washington administration gives out a trillion-dollar tax cut to the wealthy.

If the goal of our leaders continues to be regime change, then let regime change begin at home. We must be prepared to continue to provide lawful, nonviolent, civil resistance in this nation. We must be prepared to exercise our constitutionally protected rights to assemble, to free speech, to free press, to challenge the government in the streets, on campuses, in town halls, in labor halls, in churches, wherever people gather, wherever people meet, in a manner consistent with the finest democratic traditions.

If we are successful in disarming Iraq nonviolently, then our nation needs to hasten our efforts to lead the way for disarmament worldwide. Seventeen nations are seeking, have, or are capable of acquiring nuclear weapons of mass destruction, twenty nations biological weapons, twenty-six nations chemical weapons.

Over twenty nations have or are at work on missile technologies to deliver those weapons. America has much work to do as a nation among nations, furthering peace through disarmament.

We are at a transformational opportunity in this nation. It is no less significant than the spirit of the times which gave birth to this nation over two hundred and twenty-six years ago.

In his exploration of the philosophical underpinnings of America, in a work entitled *To Begin the World Anew,* Bernard Bailyn writes of that long ago moment of democratic ferment which produced the world's grandest experiment with democracy through ". . . the recasting of the world of power, the re-formation of the structure of public authority, of the accepted forms of governance, obedience, and resistance, in practice as well as in theory."

Such was the creativity of our founders. They used the creative energy of their hearts and spirits to change the world. Why has our creativity turned destructive? We need no longer be destructive with war. It is time to be creative in peace.

Dr. Martin Luther King had a dream. It is time to make his dream a reality. It is time to take the evolutionary life of Dr. King and make non-violence an organizing principle in our society. It is the practical and pragmatic thing to do in order to continue life on this planet. We can do so. And we must do so. Legislation to create a Department of Peace would build not only a structure for peace within our government, but infuse a consciousness for peace within our society, as has the Department of Defense reflected a consciousness of war.

It is time to create new possibilities in human relations, in economics, in governance, in politics and in all areas of endeavor. We can make war and poverty archaic and usher in a new era of human dignity by making peace and prosperity our daily work.

This day is a day to reflect on the ability of one person to make a difference. This day is a day to reflect on how one person can change the thinking of a nation and the world. This day is to celebrate our human potential to transform any condition, to change darkness into light, slavery into freedom, poverty into prosperity, war into peace. Let us honor America's apostle of non-violence by truly rededicating ourselves to his work. Let us make the vision of Dr. King, that vision of liberty and harmony, a reality. Let us confirm our commitment to all civil rights and let us declare peace a civil right in a democracy, a human right in this world.

Adapted from a speech given at the Lakewood Ministerial Alliance Martin Luther King Day Celebration, Lakewood Presbyterian Church, Sunday, January 19, 2003 Lakewood, Ohio

Peace and Nuclear Disarmament

"Come my friends, 'tis not too late to seek a newer world"

—Alfred, Lord Tennyson

If you believe that humanity has a higher destiny, if you believe we can evolve, and become better than we are; if you believe we can overcome the scourge of war and someday fulfill the dream of harmony and peace on earth, let us begin the conversation today. Let us exchange our ideas. Let us plan together, act together, and create peace together. This is a call for common sense, for peaceful, nonviolent citizen action to protect our precious world from widening war and from stumbling into a nuclear catastrophe.

The climate for conflict has intensified, with the struggle between Pakistan and India, the China-Taiwan tug of war, and the increased bloodshed between Israel and the Palestinians. The United States' troop deployments in the Philippines, Yemen, Georgia, Columbia, and Indonesia create new possibilities for expanded war. An invasion of Iraq is planned. The recent disclosure that Russia, China, Iraq, Iran, Syria, North Korea, and Libya are considered by the United States as possible targets for nuclear attack catalyzes potential conflicts everywhere.

These crucial political decisions promoting increased military actions, plus a new nuclear first-use policy, are occurring without the consent of the American people, without public debate, without public hearings, without public votes. The President is taking Congress's approval of responding to the September 11 terrorists as a license to flirt with nuclear war.

"Politics ought to stay out of fighting a war," the President has been quoted as saying on March 13, 2002. Yet Article 1, Section 8 of the United States Constitution explicitly requires that Congress take responsibility when it comes to declaring war. This president is very popular, according to the polls. But polls are not a substitute for democratic process. Attributing a negative connotation here to politics or dismissing constitutionally mandated congressional oversight belies reality. Spending $400 billion a year for defense is a political decision. Committing troops abroad is a political decision. War is a political decision. When men and women die on the battlefield, that is the result of a political decision. The use of nuclear weapons, which can end the lives of millions, is a profound political decision. In a monarchy there need be no political decisions. In a democracy, all decisions are political, in that they derive from the consent of the governed.

In a democracy, budgetary, military, and national objectives must be subordinate to the political process. Before we celebrate an imperial presidency, let it be said that the lack of free and open political process, the lack of free and open political debate, and the lack of free and open political dissent can be fatal in a democracy.

We have reached a moment in our country's history when it is urgent that people everywhere speak out as president of his or her own life, to protect the peace of the nation and world within and without. We should speak out and caution leaders who generate fear through talk of the endless war or the final conflict. We should appeal to our leaders to consider that their own bellicose thoughts, words, and deeds are reshaping consciousness and can have an adverse effect on our nation. Because when one person thinks *fight!* he or she finds a fight. One faction thinks *war!* and starts a war. One nation thinks *nuclear!* and approaches the abyss. And what of one nation which thinks peace, and seeks peace?

Neither individuals nor nations exist in a vacuum, which is why we have a serious responsibility for each other in this world. It is also urgent that we find those places of war in our own lives, and begin healing the world through healing ourselves. Each of us is a citizen of a common planet, bound to a common destiny. So connected are we that each of us has the power to be the eyes of the world, the voice of the world, the conscience of the world, or the end of the world. And as each one of us chooses, so becomes the world.

Each of us is architect of this world. Our thoughts, the concepts. Our words, the designs. Our deeds, the bricks and mortar of our daily lives. Which is why we should always take care to regard the power of our thoughts and words, and the commands they send into action through time and space.

Some of our leaders have been thinking and talking about nuclear war. In the past week there has been much news about a planning document which describes how and when America might wage nuclear war. The Nuclear Posture Review recently released to the media by the government:

1. Assumes that the United States has the right to launch a preemptive nuclear strike.
2. Equates nuclear weapons with conventional weapons.
3. Attempts to minimize the consequences of the use of nuclear weapons.
4. Promotes nuclear response to a chemical or biological attack.

Some dismiss this review as routine government planning. But it becomes ominous when taken in the context of a war on terrorism which keeps expanding its boundaries, rhetorically and literally. The president equates the "war on terrorism" with World War II. He expresses a desire to have the nuclear option "on the table." He unilaterally withdraws from the ABM Treaty. He seeks $8.9 billion to fund deployment of a missile shield. He institutes, without congressional knowledge, a shadow government in a bunker outside our nation's Capitol. He tries to pass off as arms reduction the storage of, instead of the elimination of, nuclear weapons.

Two generations ago we lived with nuclear night-mares. We feared and hated the Russians who feared and hated us. We feared and hated the "godless, atheistic" communists. In our schools, we dutifully put our head between our legs and practiced duck-and-cover drills. In our nightmares, we saw the long, slow arc of a Soviet mis-sile flash into our very neighborhood. We got down on our knees and prayed for peace. We surveyed, wide eyed, pictures of the destruction of Nagasaki and Hiroshima. We supported the elimination of all nuclear weapons. We knew that if you "nuked" others, you "nuked" yourself.

The splitting of the atom for destructive purposes admits a split consciousness, the compartmentalized thinking of Us versus Them, the dichotomized thinking, which spawns polarity and leads to war. The proposed use of nuclear weapons pollutes the psyche with the arro-gance of infinite power. It creates delusions of domination of matter and space. It is dehumanizing through its cal-culations of mass casualties. We must overcome doom-thinkers and sayers who invite a world descending, disintegrating into a nuclear disaster. With a world at risk, we must find the bombs in our own lives and disarm them. We must listen to that quiet inner voice which counsels that the survival of all is achieved through the unity of all.

We must overcome our fear of each other by seeking out the humanity within each of us. The human heart contains every possibility of race, creed, language, reli-gion, and politics. We are one in our commonalities. Must we always fear our differences? We can overcome our fears by not feeding our fears with more war and nuclear confrontations. We must ask our leaders to unify us in courage.

We need to create a new, clear vision of a world as one. A new, clear vision of people working out their differences peacefully. A new, clear vision with the teaching of nonviolence, nonviolent intervention, and mediation. A new, clear vision where people can live in harmony within their families, their communities, and within themselves. A new, clear vision of peaceful coexistence in a world of tolerance.

At this moment of peril we must move away from fear's paralysis. This is a call to action to replace expanded war with expanded peace. This is a call for action to place the very survival of this planet on the agenda of all people, everywhere. As citizens of a common planet, we have an obligation to ourselves and our posterity. We must demand that our nation and all nations put down the nuclear sword. We must demand that our nation and all nations:

- Abide by the principles of the nuclear Non-Proliferation Treaty.
- Stop the development of new nuclear weapons.
- Take all nuclear weapons systems off alert.
- Persist towards total, worldwide elimination of all nuclear weapons.

Our nation must:

- Revive the Anti-Ballistic Missile Treaty.
- Sign and enforce the Comprehensive Test Ban Treaty.
- Abandon plans to build a so-called missile shield.
- Prohibit the introduction of weapons into outer space.

We are in a climate where people expect debate within our two party system to produce policy alternatives. However, both major political parties have fallen short. People who ask "Where is the Democratic Party?" and expect to hear debate may be disappointed. When peace is not on the agenda of our political parties or our governments, then it must be the work and the duty of each citizen of the world. This is the time to organize for peace. This is the time for new thinking. This is the time to conceive of peace as not simply being the absence of violence, but the active presence of the capacity for a higher evolution of human awareness. This is the time to conceive of peace as respect, trust, and integrity. This is the time to tap the infinite capabilities of humanity to transform consciousness which compels violence at a personal, group, national, or international level. This is the time to develop a new compassion for others and ourselves.

When terrorists threaten our security, we must enforce the law and bring terrorists to justice within our system of constitutional justice, without undermining the very civil liberties which permit our democracy to breathe. Our own instinct for life, which inspires our breath and informs our pulse, excites our capacity to reason. Which is why we must pay attention when we sense a threat to survival.

That is why we must speak out now to protect this nation, all nations, and the entire planet and:

- Challenge those who believe that war is inevitable.
- Challenge those who believe in a nuclear right.
- Challenge those who would build new nuclear weapons. Challenge those who seek nuclear re-armament.
- Challenge those who seek nuclear escalation.
- Challenge those who would make of any nation a nuclear target.
- Challenge those who would threaten to use nuclear weapons against civilian populations.
- Challenge those who would break nuclear treaties.
- Challenge those who think and think about nuclear weapons to think about peace.

It is practical to work for peace. I speak of peace and diplomacy not just for the sake of peace itself. But, for practical reasons, we must work for peace as a means of achieving permanent security. It is similarly practical to work for total nuclear disarmament, particularly when nuclear arms do not even come close to addressing the real security problems which confront our nation—witness the events of September 11, 2001.

We can make war archaic. Skeptics may dismiss the possibility that a nation which spends $400 billion a year for military purposes can somehow convert swords into plowshares. Yet the very founding and the history of this country demonstrates the creative possibilities of America. We are a nation which is known for realizing impossible dreams. Ours is a nation which in its second century abolished slavery, which many at the time considered impossible. Ours is a nation where women won the right to vote, which many at the time considered impossible. Ours is a nation which institutionalized the civil rights movement, which many at the time considered impossible. If we have the courage to claim peace, with the passion, the emotion, and the integrity with which we have claimed independence, freedom, and equality, we can become that nation which makes nonviolence an organizing principle in our society, and in doing so change the world.

That is the purpose of HR 2459. It is a bill to create a Department of Peace. It envisions new structures to help create peace in our homes, in our families, in our schools, in our neighborhoods, in our cities, and in our nation. It aspires to create conditions for peace within and to create conditions for peace worldwide. It considers the conditions which cause people to become the terrorists of the future—issues of poverty, scarcity, and exploitation. It is practical to make outer space safe from weapons, so that humanity can continue to pursue a destiny among the stars. HR 3616 seeks to ban weapons in space, to keep the stars a place of dreams, of new possibilities, of transcendence.

We can achieve this practical vision of peace, if we are ready to work for it. People worldwide need to meet with like-minded people, about peace and nuclear disarmament, now. People worldwide need to gather in peace, now. People worldwide need to march and to pray for peace, now. People worldwide need to be connecting with each other on the Web, for peace, now. We are in a new era of electronic democracy, where the World Wide Web, with its numerous websites and bulletin boards, enable new organizations, exercising freedom of speech, freedom of assembly, and freedom of association, to spring into being instantly. *Thespiritoffreedom.com* is such a website. It is dedicated to becoming an electronic forum for peace, for sustainability, for renewal, and for revitalization. It is a forum which strives for the restoration of a sense of community through the empowerment of self, through commitment of self to the lives of others, to the life of the community, to the life of the nation, to the life of the world.

Where war making is profoundly uncreative in its destruction, peacemaking can be deeply creative. We need to communicate with each other about the ways in which we can work in our communities to make this a more peaceful world. I welcome your ideas at: *dkucinich@aol.com*.

We can share our thoughts and discuss ways in which we have brought or will bring them into action. Now is the time to think, to take action, and use our talents and abilities to create peace:

- In our families.
- In our block clubs.
- In our neighborhoods.
- In our places of worship.
- In our schools and universities.
- In our labor halls.
- In our parent-teacher organizations.

Now is the time to think, speak, write, organize, and take action to create peace as a social imperative, as an economic imperative, and as a political imperative. Now is the time to think, speak, write, organize, march, rally, hold vigils, and take other nonviolent action to create peace in our cities, in our nation, and in the world. And as the hymn says, "Let there be peace on earth and let it begin with me."

This is the work of the human family, of people all over the world demanding that governments and non-governmental actors alike put down their nuclear weapons. This is the work of the human family, responding in this moment of crisis to protect our nation, this planet, and all life within it. We can achieve both nuclear disarmament and peace. As we understand that all people of the world are interconnected, we can achieve both nuclear disarmament and peace. We can accomplish this through upholding a holistic vision where the claims of all living beings to the right of survival are recognized. We can achieve both nuclear disarmament and peace through being a living testament to a Human Rights

Covenant, where each person on this planet is entitled to a life where he or she may consciously evolve in mind, body, and spirit.

Nuclear disarmament and peace are the signposts toward the uplifting path of an even brighter human condition wherein we can, through our conscious efforts, evolve and reestablish the context of our existence from peril to peace, from revolution to evolution. Think peace. Speak peace. Act peace. Peace.

Adapted from a speech to the House of Representatives, March 20, 2002

WORK
AND
HEALTH

THE SOUL OF THE WORKER

My father was a teamster, and so I was literally born into the House of Labor, as were my six brothers and sisters. As the oldest child, I was also the first to have a job. Though being employed doesn't solve all of a family's problems—our family had lived in twenty-one different places by the time I was seventeen. One of my first jobs was at the *Plain Dealer* newspaper in Cleveland. As a copyboy I joined the American Newspaper Guild. Years later, working at TV 8, I belonged to American Federation of Television & Radio Artists (AFTRA). Today I am a member of the cameraman's union, the International Alliance of Theatrical and Stage Employees (IATSE) of the American Foundations of Labor-Congress of Industrial Organizations (AFL-CIO). As for my father, he drove a truck for thirty-five years, and died with his first retirement check in his pocket, uncashed.

I am of the House of Labor, and that house is still being built. I carry my membership card for the House of

Representatives, where my work is. My IATSE card is where my heart is.

The hopes and dreams of the men and women who sent me to Congress are the stars by which I journey. Whenever there is an organizing campaign, a picket line to walk, jobs to save, working conditions to improve, laws to champion, I'm there. This is my purpose: to stand up and speak out on behalf of those who have built this country and on behalf of those who want to rebuild this country. This is my passion, since I believe that workers' rights are the key to protecting our democracy.

Workers' rights embody spiritual principles that sustain families, nourish the soul, and create peace. Workers' rights are human rights.

Today, let us rededicate our efforts to bring economic justice to those who have created the wealth through their work. A re-energized labor movement will re-energize America's politics and create a more just society. The cause of union, of brotherhood and sisterhood, is felt in the workers' anthem. Solidarity can be the song that echoes across this land. It can be the music that lifts up the hearts of all those who dignify work with their toil.

For decades, labor has been telling the nation about the dangers of unchecked corporate power. Organizing campaigns have brought the lessons home. Employers are firing union supporters; forcing workers to listen to anti-union propaganda from company supervisors; bringing in outsiders to run well-funded anti-union campaigns threatening loss of jobs and even threatening to move out of town.

Labor stands alone in many of its struggles and we need to change this. We need a Democratic Party that will insure the right to organize by establishing an automatic union once half the workers sign up. When workers can choose a union, free of fear and intimidation, they choose to have the collective voice a union provides. As a member of the Cleveland Jobs With Justice workers' rights board, I have seen the community help nearly two thousand workers to join unions. We need a national labor law that provides for democracy in the workplace.

Labor has stood almost alone while corporations have cut wages and benefits, slashed working hours, tried to undermine wage and hour provisions, reneged on contracts, and jettisoned retirements through bankruptcy strategies. The current clamor for corporate accountability calls for honesty in stating the numbers, and faithful custody of shareholders' money.

Yet there needs to be equal concern for those who created the wealth through their labor, since the attacks on unions are a means of redistributing the wealth upward. As union membership has declined, the disparity between rich and poor has increased. Since 1973, union membership has dropped from twenty-four percent to fourteen percent, and during that same period the share of aggregate income of the poor, the middle class, and the upper middle class has also declined.

It's an old saying that the rich get richer. But it's a new convention in the American political economy that a class of working poor has emerged, including the working homeless. Congress has not passed an increase in the $5.15 minimum wage even though the inflation-adjusted minimum wage is twenty-one percent lower today than it was in 1979.

Since 1981, the share of income of the richest 5 percent of this country has increased by more than 40 percent while that of the lowest fifth has decreased by more than 20 percent. An even starker contrast was reported in *Business Week*: The average CEO made forty-two times the average worker's pay in 1980, eighty-five times in 1990, and 531 times in 2000. *Forbes* magazine points out that the number of billionaires increased from thirteen in 1982 to 149 in 1996.

Over the past twenty years, whenever labor sat at the negotiating table, it fought for fair wages and benefits and was told it was just asking for too much, that the demands would make the company less competitive. And all the while the wealth kept getting accelerated upward, with the help of NAFTA and other trade agreements that were designed to undermine workers' rights and lower wages worldwide.

Over one hundred years ago, Pope Leo XIII wrote in his encyclical "Rerum Novarum":

Working men have been surrendered, isolated and helpless, to the hardheartedness of employers and the greed of unchecked competition. . . . The hiring of labor and the conduct of trade are concentrated in the hands of comparatively few; so that a small number of very rich men have been able to lay upon the teeming masses of the laboring poor a yoke little better than that of slavery itself.

I quote a great spiritual leader because supporting efforts to lift up the human condition through improving standards of work is a great moral cause. It is about the intrinsic worth of each and every human being. When work and workers are valued, when all men and women are given a chance to earn their daily bread, when all are paid a living wage, when hands strong and weak can clasp in common enterprise to seek and to build a newer world—then every day will belong to the workers. And every voice will praise the moment when human toil has lifted up the human condition. It is a noble cause that brings us together, and that is why we put ourselves on the line.

We need to feel in every cell of our bodies the power that comes from union: the power that confirms our purpose, the power that, when focused and directed, will save our nation by saving the Democratic Party from the clutches of corporate interests. Enlightened self-interest requires Labor to make the Democratic Party accountable. Labor must rally the Democrats to the workers' banner. Labor must begin now to build the Democratic Party platform for 2004 to insure that solid principles of economic justice prevail, and to inspire millions of Americans, who would otherwise stay home on Election Day, to vote to save our democracy.

Labor cannot afford to settle for half-hearted nominees

or half-measures that keep in place a system that is destroying our democracy through trade agreements that transfer sovereign power to the World Trade Organization, undermine our economy, and devastate workers' ability to defend themselves. "All that harms labor is treason," said President Lincoln. "If any man tells you that he loves America [but] he hates labor, he is a liar." Supporters of the decaying system of injustice continue to advance propositions that are an offense to basic fairness and workers' dignity. With the Team Act they attacked the right to organize. With the Rewarding Performance in Compensation Act, they wanted to strip workers of overtime. In the name of workplace flexibility, they wanted to repeal the Fair Labor Standards Act. With the Paycheck Protection Act they attacked union dues as compulsory and political. They wanted workplace safety rules set by corporate consensus and not by OSHA. They would take us back to the days when workers had no protections or rights. Back to the days of "Sixteen Tons."

"You load sixteen tons, and what do you get? Another day older and deeper in debt. St. Peter don't you call me, 'cause I can't go, I owe my soul to the company store."

No more sixteen tons in America! The soul of the worker is not for sale. It will not be sacrificed upon the corporate altar, nor annihilated by a hostile or indifferent government. The soul of the worker will be redeemed by the enshrinement in law of workers' rights. If in 2004 Labor goes up to the mountaintop of our nation's capital, it must bring back, engraved in stone, the rights of working people.

People have a right to a job.

A right to a safe workplace.

A right to decent wages and benefits.

A right organize and be represented.

A right to grieve about working conditions.

A right to strike.

A right to fair compensation for injuries on the job.

A right to sue if injured by negligent employers.

A right to sercurity of pension and retirement benefits.

A right to participate in the political process.

There can be no true corporate accountability unless corporations are accountable to workers. There can be no accountability to workers unless workers' rights are protected. And workers' rights cannot be protected unless the Democratic Party makes them the centerpiece of its legislative program, and its drive for the White House in 2004. The Democratic Party must be challenged by labor to truly be the party of all the people.

When the Democratic Party rises it must be with the ranks, not from the ranks. "The future of labor is the future of America," said John L. Lewis.

The restoration of the rights of workers will put us at the dawn of a new political age, since those rights are core principles of an American Restoration. These aren't mere political principles; they are timeless moral principles about fairness, about equality, about justice.

The English Restoration of the 1660s brought the royal family back to power. The American Restoration will be about restoring the American working family to economic power, to insure that all have jobs, that all have meaningful work and that all make a living wage. "The enthusiasm of falling welfare numbers," said Cardinal Mahoney, "should be tempered by the reality of persistent poverty and wages too meager to provide for a family's needs. Many may be leaving welfare, too few have left poverty." Twenty-five percent of all workers in Iowa earn poverty-level hourly wages. Who can live at $5.15 an hour? The campaign for a living wage is fundamental to making certain that people have more than crumbs when they sit down to eat their daily bread.

The restoration of the rights of workers in America and throughout the North American continent will begin when we repeal the North American Free Trade Agreement. NAFTA promised new manufacturing jobs, but it has instead been devastating to the American worker. NAFTA has spurred a $360 billion trade deficit and has cost three million jobs, many of them in manufacturing. Each job lost represents dreams deferred or shattered, or a home that was threatened, health insurance that was lost, retirement benefits evaporated. This is called free trade. But where is the freedom when jobs are lost? Where is the freedom when industries threaten to move out of the country unless wages are cut? Where is the freedom when the right to collective bargaining is crushed? Where is the freedom when a union is broken? Where is the freedom when you can't make a mortgage payment? Where is the freedom when you can't send your children to college? An economic democracy is a precondition of a political democracy, not vice versa. Where is the freedom?

The NAFTA regime has attacked federal laws meant to protect worker rights, human rights, and environmental-quality principles. NAFTA promised new export markets for U.S. farm products, but that is a broken promise. The U.S. trade surplus has fallen. It is time to stop those roll-backs. It is time to reclaim state and local sovereignty, which NAFTA has usurped. No NAFTA, no fast track, and no more backtracking on workers' rights.

"The working people know no country. They are citizens of the world," said AFL-CIO founder Samuel Gompers in 1887. It is time for a return to nation-to-nation bilateral trade agreements. It is time for humane trading partnerships where the living wages, benefits, and retirement security of workers of each nation are the centerpiece of trade pacts.

The American Restoration will be about restoring the physical health of our people through universal healthcare. A market-based system of healthcare has brought about the closure of hundreds of community hospitals, has limited access to health care, denied specialized care, driven up costs, and made health care a bargaining chip in negotiations, forcing trade-offs for wage increases. This is an abomination.

But do we have the political freedom, the will, and the courage to transform a system where, for tens of millions of people, every accident and every illness carries with it the fear of being unable to afford proper treatment?

We must restore the American dream of home owner-ship through lowering and regulating lending rates, ending predatory lending practices, increasing the per-centage of the home mortgage deduction for middle-income people, and stopping home insurance redlining.

In his inagural address in 1933, Franklin Delano Roo-sevelt declared, "The practices of the unscrupulous money changers stand indicted in the court of public opinion rejected by the minds and hearts of men." Under Roosevelt the government took responsibility for the eco-nomic vitality of consumers. Today, the government pro-tects credit-card companies, banks, and insurance companies. This must change.

Our nation will be restored with a new manufacturing policy, where the maintenance of our industrial base is understood to be vital to our national economic welfare. We can fuel domestic steel production and consumption by rebuilding our nation's infrastructure with American-made steel, utilizing the productive capacity of our mills. We need to spend at least $500 billion to rebuild our schools, roads, bridges, ports, sewer systems, water sys-tems, and government buildings. A highly trained, highly skilled work force backed by Davis-Bacon guarantees will make it happen. A federal bank can be created to fund this program with zero-interest loans to the states.

America needs a new public works program to restore the dream of a full-employment economy, and to restore the physical health of our nation. Labor, inspired to rally the disaffected, the dispirited, the disenfran-chised, can provide new hope for our country through bringing forth new leadership responsive in word and deed to the task of rebuilding our nation.

A rebuilt infrastructure will help restore American commerce. This nation cannot come through the crisis of confidence in corporate America simply through improving accounting practices and imprisoning [a few] wayward executives. Our country must restore its economy by restoring competition, by breaking up monopolies, by genuine antitrust enforcement, by re-regulation, by the federal chartering of corporations, and by the repeal of Taft-Hartley, which deprives the American workplace of the right to a strong, co-equal relationship with labor. "The measure of the restoration," FDR said, "lies in the extent to which we apply social values more noble than mere monetary profit."

Antitrust enforcement is needed in all areas of the economy, especially in agriculture, where unfair practices from seed to store are driving family farmers out of business. We must free the family farmer from the market dominance of agribusiness and its predatory policies, which set prices so farmers can't survive. Americans are learning hard lessons about the dangers of monopolies in energy. When Americans learn the difference between the price the producer gets and what consumers pay for food, and when Americans realize the risks dependency on imports and corporate mega-farms bring to our national food supply, we will be on the path of reform—and that is how we will protect independent farmers.

The largest roadblock on the road to an American Restoration is a corrupt campaign financing system that promotes plutocracy, allowing laws and regulations to be stealthily auctioned to the highest bidder. Less than 1 percent of the U.S. population contributes 80 percent of the money in federal elections. The top 1 percent in income also received more than half the tax cuts. Tax policy has become an engine for transferring wealth upward. Enron was poised to dominate energy markets worldwide because it controlled the White House, and it gave to seventy-one senators and 186 House members.

Private control of campaign financing leads to private control of the government itself, and to schemes like the privatization of Social Security, which would put nearly $7 trillion in retirement funds at the disposal of Wall Street speculators over the next twenty-five years. Public control of the political process requires public financing. The restoration of our American Democracy depends on public financing. The Supreme Court, however, in equating money with free speech, will not restrict the ability of corporate interests to own the government. The establishment of our democracy began with the Constitution. Let us renew the Constitution by amending it, requiring public financing to guarantee a government of the people, by the people, and for the people.

Everyone knows that it is the sons and daughters of America's working people who are the first called into battle. It has always been that way. Except this administration has not made its case to go to war against Iraq.

Iraq was not responsible for 9/11, for Al Qaeda's role in 9/11, for the anthrax attacks on our country. Iraq does not have missile technology that would enable it to reach our shores with its weapons. And Iraq has not been shown to have usable weapons of mass destruction.

This war is wrong. It puts at risk the lives of our servicemen and servicewomen, and puts to risk the lives of innocent civilians in Iraq. Surely, everyone understands that if we kill thousands of civilians, anger against America will rise and we will become increasingly less safe here at home. We have a right to defend ourselves, but we also have an obligation not to make America less safe.

This administration, which is run by energy interests, gave a trillion-dollar tax cut to the rich and is prepared to acclerate the transfer of wealth through a war that will cost at least $200 billion and perhaps much more. There is no money for health care, no money for child care, no money for living wages, no money for Social Security, or Medicare—there is only money for tax cuts for the rich, and for war. And in the end, corporate interests will win while fresh, new graves will be dug on two continents.

The hopes of the peoples of two nations are being smashed by weapons, in the name of eliminating weapons. Let us abolish weapons of mass destruction at home. Corporate control of government is a weapon of mass destruction. Joblessness is a weapon of mass destruction. Poverty is a weapon of mass destruction. Homelessness, poor healthcare, poor education, discrimination—these all are weapons of mass destruction. We need a Worker's White house to fight against these destructive weapons.

Let us use hundreds of billions of our tax dollars instead for the restoration of the dreams of the American worker, to rebuild our economy and to expand opportunities for all. Peace will protect the rights of workers. This administration has already used the rubric of national security to try and roll back the rights of the American Federation of Government Employees. It is attempting to frustrate the efforts of airport security workers to organize. Its anti-worker agenda includes not only strikebreaking and attacking collective bargaining, it also includes cheating workers out of overtime pay.

We need a new vision of America, as a nation among nations, as a strong presence but not as king of a unipolar world dictating policy on behalf of global corporate interests. We need a vision that connects workers and all people in the highest causes of the human spirit: peace and justice. This will be the crowning achievement of an American Restoration, the liberation of people all over the world.

As we face the challenges ahead, let us recall the plea of the Prophet Isaiah: "To unlock the shackles of injustice? To break every cruel chain? Then shall your light shine in the darkness. Your people shall lay the foundations for ages to come. You shall be called repairer of the breach. Restorer of the streets to dwell in."

It is the light of the men and women of Labor that will shine in the darkness. They will lay the foundation for ages to come. They will repair the breach. They will lead the American Restoration.

Adapted from a speech given at the International Water Rights Conference, British Columbia University, Vancouver, British Columbia, July 7, 2001

Water As a Human Right

We understand, intuitively, that we are all called here today for a high purpose, so as we begin on this beautiful day, let us rededicate ourselves to the beautiful principles which have called us. Our love for each other. Our love for our common habitat, this great blue-green globe. Our love for our children and for future generations. Our belief that we have in our hands the ability to transform any system to make it more accountable, more caring, more nurturing, more intrinsically human.

Water is our sacrament. It gives us life, nourishes us, restores us physically, and refreshes us. It is a work of mercy to give water to a thirsty person and it is a work of justice to stop water from being denied to a thirsty person. Today we satisfy our thirst for justice by drinking from nature's cup. Today, on this beautiful day we anoint ourselves with a holy purpose, to safeguard the world's water for all God's creatures, and to confirm water's essentiality to our very nature.

The poet, James Russell Lowell, spoke of the natural beauty of a summer month:

> . . . then, if ever come perfect days,
> When heaven try earth if it be in tune,
> And over it softly her warm ear lays.
> Whether we look, or whether we listen,
> We hear life murmur, or see it glisten.
> Every clod feels a stir of might,
> An instinct within it
> That reaches and towers,
> And groping blindly above it for light
> Climbs to a soul in grass and flowers. . . .

Today, we see life in a single drop of water. Today, we feel a stir of might as our hearts connect with something transcendent—water for life. Today, the instinct for oneness reaches and towers within us and we reach for the light of human dignity and justice and our soul magnifies all of nature.

How grim a future where nature stands stripped bare with the curse of commodification. How dim a vision of death, of future wars being fought over water which maintains life! We are here today to declare our oneness and to shine our light through the darkness of that prophecy. We are here today to bring peace to those who countenance war over water.

Seen as a business, the global market for water will soon be worth over one trillion dollars. In this global market, water is viewed as a commodity to be traded, as a market to be captured, as a substance to be priced at whatever price the market will bear. In this water market, corporations can, as privateers, sail the bounded main and own all the water they can see.

In this market, international trade agreements, as exemplified by NAFTA, GATT, the WTO, and the proposed FTAA, guarantee corporations access to water anywhere in the world, and seek to make government resources, and tax dollars, available to those who wish to privatize water systems and other public service facilities.

Under privatization, water is priced according to "the willingness and ability to pay." Seen from this perspective, water is a good business. The demand is constant and thirsty people are willing to pay as much as they are willing to live.

In the lowest income countries, people pay a wholly disproportionate share of their income to private water companies. This leads to an intensification of the disparities between rich and poor countries. Just how did private water companies make it to Benin, Honduras, Nicaragua, Niger, Panama, Rwanda, Tanzania, and other poor nations? They have had their access delivered by the IMF and the World Bank.

In order to fully understand the crisis facing third world countries, consider this: The International Monetary Fund and the World Bank view government subsidy of water as creating a deficit and demands a country achieve "full cost recovery" for its water. This means even prior to privatization, a nation wanting assistance from the IMF or World Bank must increase its water rates.

The IMF and the World Bank have imposed loan conditions on many countries, which have required:

1. Water rate increases.
2. Eventual privatization of the nation's water system, which means
3. More water rate increases.

Under this miserable ethic, the people of third world countries end up as sharecroppers working the water plantation, working just to get their share of water to live. It is axiomatic that without water there is no life. Poor people are forced into cruel trade-offs, water or food, water or health care. We come to a moment where it is fair to observe that either the people own water or water will own the people.

Perhaps as never before the benefits and the necessity of public ownership become manifest.

Under public ownership:

Universal service is required to urban and rural areas.
There is a requirement to serve all people, regardless of their income.
There is a political incentive to establish service at the lowest possible price.
There is a requirement of public accountability.
There is a requirement to seek public approval for policy changes and for rate increases.
There is a requirement to manage water systems in cooperation with the environment and in consideration for impact on public health.
Everyone is a shareholder in the commonwealth of public ownership.

Contrast this with the role of private ownership:

> The purpose of private ownership is to make a profit.
> Profits must be sufficient to guarantee a solid rate of
> return for investors.
> The incentive is to establish service at the highest pos-
> sible price.
> Pricing will be at whatever the market will bear.
> The growth of the company is of paramount concern.

It should be clear that when it comes to providing the essentials of life, such as an affordable, accessible supply of drinking water, the interests of the public sector and the private sector are mutually exclusive, whether within local, national, or international structures.

Today is an appropriate day to recommend a series of declarative statements which can serve as the basis for a course of action. We shall call these ten principles "Water Marks":

1. All water shall be considered to be forever in the public domain.
2. It shall be the duty of each nation to provide accessible, affordable drinking water to its people.
3. There shall be public ownership of drinking water systems, subject to municipal control.
4. Wealthy nations shall provide poor nations with the means to obtain water for survival.
5. Water shall be protected from commodification and exempted from all trade agreements.

6. Water privatization shall not be a condition of debt restructuring, loan renewal, or loan forgiveness.
7. Governments shall use their powers to prevent private aggregation of water rights.
8. Water shall be conserved through sustainable agriculture and encouraging plant-based diets.
9. Water resources shall be protected from pollution.
10. Our children should be educated about the essential nature of water for maintaining life.

Globalization must be preceded by global recognition of basic human rights. Otherwise people exist for the marketplace instead of the marketplace existing for the people. The UN Declaration of Human Rights, as set forth on December 10, 1948, declares in Article I that "All human beings are born free and equal in dignity and rights." Access to water is essential to assuring human dignity. Article 3 of the UN Declaration closely mirrors the insistence of America's own Declaration of Independence: "Everyone has a right to life, liberty, and security of person." Water is a precondition for life; therefore it is a basic human right. It is our duty, as citizens of a common planet, to work cooperatively to assure that this right is guaranteed to each and every person, regardless of his or her economic status or the economic status of the nation in which they live.

Adapted from a speech given at the International Water Rights Conference, British Columbia University, Vancouver, British Columbia, July 7, 2001

THE HEALTH OF OUR NATION

Health care is a special vocation. I know because I worked at Saint Alexis Hospital in Cleveland, Ohio as an orderly and as a surgical technician. My experience took me to every part of the hospital and every part of the patient. I scrubbed floors, worked in the emergency room, ran the cast cart, and transported patients. I learned total patient care, full baths, cleaning bed pans, making up the bed, charting vital signs, input and output, delivering meals, answering the call whenever a patient's light went on. In surgery, I folded laundry, prepared the instruments to be used in the operation, worked as first scrub on every kind of case. At Saint Alexis, I was present at that incredible moment when people pass from life to death, and at those equally awesome times when, because of the skill of doctors, nurses, and staff, life is rescued and restored.

I punched the clock and sometimes I felt like the clock punched me. When you work in a health care facility, each day challenges you physically, emotionally, and spiritually. But you do it because you love people. The personal satisfactions are many. You feel a special sense of purpose when you are part of a team which gives people help and comfort when they need it. Because of your efforts each place you work is made special. Whatever your job in health care, you represent and you communicate timeless healing principles of caring, of consideration, of kindness, of touch.

Health care workers know the power of a smile to the suffering and the lonely, the importance of offering assistance to help someone to eat to nourish recovery, the meaning of a hand extended to help someone walk after suffering a disability. This is what I experienced when I worked at Saint Alexis, participating in a community of health care servants who felt special, as all such communities are special.

You chose the profession which helps the blind see, the lame walk, the heart regain its strength, the body regain its resolve, the spirit regain its energy. You see the work of technology as it enables lives to be rescued. Each new day brings you near the pageant of life and death. Each new day confirms a deeper meaning of life. Each new day is one of miracles. Miracles of technology. Miracles of faith. Miracles of hope. And you are witness to this each and every day. Thank you for the work that you do. Thank you for your commitment. Thank you for caring not only to represent the Service Employees International Union members. Thank you for the commitment of the SEIU in representing the interests of the patients.

Your members are attuned not only to the health of

the system of the individual patients, they are attuned to the health of the healthcare system, whether it lives up to its responsibility to give quality care. You know the staffing levels. You see firsthand the shortcomings of a system that understaffs health care institutions. Your members experience the pressures of wanting to deliver quality care and not having enough time to get to all the patients, of staffing limitations which lead to pressure to work longer hours which inevitably puts patients at risk. You know why people choose health care as a career and, once in it, you know why some choose not to continue.

You know the problems in health care, you know the potential of health care. You are advocates of health care workers. The interests of patients and the interests of caregivers are the same: quality health care, a well-trained and a well-paid staff.

It is your determination as advocates which has helped to rally states and the nation to the cause of patients' rights: for the doctor of choice, for full information disclosure of conditions, for specialized care when needed, and for better wages, benefits, and improved conditions for health care workers which in turn assures quality health care and keeps health care from becoming a soulless province.

As you help to protect the health care of the patient, so you are called upon to protect the health care of the nation. You, the leaders of the SEIU, are needed in a great cause to rally not only your membership, but to inspire all of labor to join in the effort to create a national health care system. Health care should not be left to the marketplace. Let us declare health care as a basic human right. It is the moral responsibility of a government in a democratic society to ensure the health of its people.

It is a sad commentary on national priorities that while corporate profits soared in America in the 1990s, by the end of that decade 39 million people were without health care. Last year another two million lost health insurance because of unemployment. Years ago, a job meant financial security and health benefits. Today a job means, well, a job, for a time. Many employers do not offer health insurance. Or the cost of health insurance offered is prohibitive. The number of uninsured persons in working families is approaching 32 million. These are persons who earn too much to qualify for government health assistance.

Mirroring the economic disparities which continue to be a painful part of our national experience, African Americans and Latinos have less access to a regular health care provider, see a doctor less often, and have less access to specialists.

You and I know that when people do not have health insurance, they wait longer to receive treatment. We know these people. They are our mothers and fathers, our sons and daughters, our brothers and sisters. They can't hear us when we say, "Go to a doctor. Go to the hospital." Because uppermost in their mind is "I don't have the money. I can't pay." The Institute of Medicine claims eighteen thousand persons die prematurely each year as a result of not having health care coverage. And millions more cannot enjoy the quality of life they have worked to obtain because of debilitating illness which remains untreated. And for those who wait until they have to be rushed to the emergency room, the system will generally recover the cost from taxpayers, consumers, or other employers through higher premiums.

The late Joseph Cardinal Bernardin said: "Now is the time for real health care reform. For many it is literally a matter of life and death, of lives cut short and dignity denied. We urge our national leaders to look beyond special interest claims and partisan differences to unite our nation in a new commitment."

Today is the time to make the new commitment. Because each day brings news of premiums being increased, of industries being shut down, of pension and health benefits being rescinded or cancelled. Americans are being crushed by a system which is pricing them out of health care, casting them out of work, and even leaving them with no unemployment insurance. One million, seven hundred thousand jobs have been lost since March of 2001. The unemployment rate stands at 5.9 percent. Soon there will be almost 900,000 unemployed workers left with no unemployment insurance, over 10 percent of them living in California. Unless unemployment and COBRA benefits are soon extended, more pressures will come upon more families, more illnesses will arise, more lives will be ruined, more dreams will be destroyed.

The economy is slowing down, wage increases are

slowing down, and the cost of health insurance is accelerating, causing more pressure on workers and taking up a larger share of family budgets. According to the National Coalition on Health Care, a little more than a decade ago a family of four would spend about $2,500 annually, or 12 percent of its budget, on health care. Today that amount is $7,000 or up to 25 percent. Health insurance premiums went up 11 percent last year, will go up 13 percent this year. Calpers, your state employee benefit program, will see a 25 percent increase in health care premiums next year.

You know the effect on your members. Health care is often the bargaining issue. Employers are passing on rising costs through copayments and deductibles which prices more and more working people out of quality health care. And if you are looking into the sunset after a lifetime of hard work, what happens to your pension when the cost of health care goes up?

Compounding the cruelty of this system is that senior citizens on Social Security have taken to using credit cards to pay for increased cost of medical care and for the skyrocketing cost of prescription drugs. As a result, more senior citizens are filing for bankruptcy than ever before. According to a Harvard University study of seniors in economic crisis,[2] 82,000 senior citizens filed for bankruptcy last year, up 244 percent from a decade ago. Half the people who filed for bankruptcy in 1999 did so because of health care bills; many are middle class families

2. "Consumer bankruptcy project" study, Harvard University, 2002.

burdened by catastrophic medical costs compounded by the possibility of losing everything one works for in a lifetime, including a home, to carry a lifetime burden of debt because of serious illness or injury. Congress's answer in so-called bankruptcy reform legislation has been to reject efforts to give relief to those with such debt.

The American health care system does not exist for us. We exist for it. "Of all the forms of inequality, injustice in health care is the most shocking and inhumane," said Martin Luther King, Jr. South Africa broke the shackles of apartheid and declared in its 1996 constitution, "Everyone has a right to have access to health care services. . . ." It is time for America to break the shackles of a system which has turned managed care into managed money and put the maintenance of profit above the maintenance of human health. Japan now has universal health care. Canada has universal health care.

"Few areas of human concern are as subject to the profound social and cultural changes affecting contemporary life as health care," said Pope John Paul II. Health care is a matter of human dignity. Health care is a matter of the common good. Health care ought to be one of the blessings of liberty. A government which derives its legitimacy from arms and force while the basic needs of the people of this nation are wanting needs to be stirred by conscience and by action. This is our challenge and let this be our cause, to repair *the health of our nation* and its people, to establish health care as a basic human right through creating single payer, universal health care in the United States.

We must replace the managed care and insurance industry which is holding doctors, patients, and the health care system itself captive. We are already paying for national health care. We are spending for it. We are not getting it. Government expenditures account for nearly 60 percent of health care costs. Our government spends more per capita than any nation except Switzerland. We spend $1.4 trillion, a larger percent of our Gross Domestic Product (14 percent) for health care than nations that have national health insurance.

The General Accounting Office in Washington has written "If the U.S. were to shift to a system of universal coverage and a single payer, as in Canada, the savings in administrative costs would be more than enough to offset the expense of universal coverage." A 7.7 percent payroll tax paid by the employer together with existing government spending for health would provide sufficient financing. We could put in place a single government fund which pays all medical expenses. A single fund which provides singular protection against illness and hopelessness. A single fund which will strengthen our families and our businesses and will enable you to go back to the bargaining table to win those wage increases which are essential to a better life.

And this is just the first step of the transformation of our health care system. The SEIU has always been willing to be at the forefront of efforts to make the health care system work. As we institute a quantitative reform of national health care, we must assist in a qualitative transformation of the entire health care system. You and your members are essential to this goal. The future of health care depends upon new cooperation between parties in the system from the moment someone needs help to the patient's journey through the system to follow-up care. The SEIU can help develop new paths. Prepare for the moment. It is upon us.

It is upon us. And it requires our active participation. The health of our nation depends not only on the health system, it also depends upon the health of unions—on your ability to organize, to bargain collectively, to get decent wages and benefits for your members, on the right to strike, on the right to get compensated fairly when injured on the job, on the right to participate in the political process.

The day I was elected to Congress, hundreds of members of the SEIU, on their own time, were canvassing door to door, making phone calls, working the polls, getting out the vote. I won by three percentage points the first time, and by fifty percentage points in the last election because the SEIU and other unions made it happen with direct voter contact.

The SEIU was there three years ago when Cleveland's largest health care system decided to close two community hospitals. Departments were closed. Emergency rooms shut. Patients transferred. We worked closely together in a great civic crusade, a coalition of doctors, nurses, and health care staff and the entire Cleveland political and labor movement saved the hospitals.

We rallied, we marched, we prayed, we went to county and federal courts. Hundreds of community hospitals have been lost in mergers, acquisitions and bankruptcies. But there are two which did not die. They are in the Cleveland area. One of them is that hospital I worked at many years ago. I remembered the community of health care workers which made Saint Alexis what it was then, what it is now as Saint Michael's, and what it will be in the future. I remembered the people I worked with, the doctors, the nurses, the staff, who love health care, who love the patients, and who love each other. It was a victory for the SEIU and for the community. Some said it was a miracle and call it "The Miracle on Broadway," for the street on which the hospital is located.

The SEIU has helped to save hospitals. Now you are called upon to help save the entire health system of a nation. When leaders such as yourself tap your own creative potential for rallying your members for a wide range of causes, anything is possible. The action is with the members. And it is out in the community, with the people, with miracles in the street. Miracles are waiting to be called forth. The miracles are inside of you. The labor movement itself is awaiting transformation. Our political system is awaiting transformation. We need a miracle. We need the SEIU.

Speech given to Service Employees International Leadership Conference, Oakland, California, Saturday, September 14, 2002

ON REPRODUCTIVE RIGHTS

Control of the Congress, the White House, and by power of appointment, the federal judiciary, has occurred at a time when the national Republican Party has pledged to enact legislation that would criminalize abortion. It has committed to an increasingly aggressive campaign. In recognition of this, I have found that the abortion-related legislation being brought to the House floor no longer reflects my position. Last year, I withheld my support from a number of bills.

I don't believe in abortion. I do, however, believe in choice.

I have always believed in the goal of reducing the need for abortions. Throughout my career, I have supported programs with this intent. I have supported social programs, expanded Medicaid coverage and maternal and child nutrition programs to strengthen vulnerable families. Also, I have stood behind programs that teach sex education, domestic family planning, and promote the use of contraception. It was my hope that these efforts would give women the information and support that they would need to make their own reproductive choices.

The decision to terminate a pregnancy is one of the most serious decisions a woman might make. It is deeply personal. In our society, all women and all men have a right to make difficult moral decisions and make personal choices. But women will not be equal to men if this constitutionally protected right is denied.

I believe that women have the right to determine their reproductive choices, and I believe that criminalizing abortion is unconstitutional. Increasingly, the bills that have been brought to the House floor would criminalize abortion or eliminate women's reproductive rights. I have never favored a constitutional amendment to criminalize abortion. I do not believe that Roe v. Wade should be overturned.

At this very moment, members of Congress are preparing to dismantle this constitutional protection. I refuse to participate in this effort. The law has the potential to keep abortion legal and safe—or make it more expensive and more dangerous.

This is a moment in history when our country is in need of conciliation, not division. I believe it is possible to stand in defense of the Constitution and, at the same time, strive to reduce the need for abortions. It is my intent to remain committed to working with all parties in this debate.

I support the Constitution, and I support a woman's right to freedom of choice.

Adapted from a speech given on February 21, 2003 in Washington D.C.

TAKING
BACK
AMERICA

Take Back America

You are wondering why I am running for president and how I will become the nominee of this party? My name is hard to pronounce. Kucinich. K-U-C-I-N-I-C-H—as in the Web site www.Kucinich.US. I have an admission. It wasn't always Kucinich. It used to be Smith. I changed it for the ethnic vote, and to bring back the Reagan Democrats.

Two days before I filed at the FEC [Federal Election Commission] I had 2 percent in the polls. Since no one knows who I am, I can only go up. And money? With me, money is no object, because it has never been the subject. But after people hear what I have to say, I expect millions of people will contact my Web site at Kucinich.US to contribute to my campaign.

I come from a state that sent the last person from the House of Representatives to the White House over one hundred twenty-two years ago. But with Global Climate Change, look at how many of these hundred-year storms are happening recently. I was told before I started it would be a cold and snowy day in hell before a liberal Democrat made it back to the White House. Yet the moment I began my campaign last week, sure enough, freezing temperatures and blizzard conditions hit from Iowa to Washington D.C. It is the sign we have all been waiting for. I tell you I am ready, so is this party, and so is America. We will replace Crawford Texas' square dancing, tractor pulls, and pork rinds with Cleveland's polka, bowling, and kielbasa. Cleveland, the new face of America. Kucinich.US. Think about it.

Of course we have other things to think about this morning. The world is on the brink of war initiated by our own government against a nation which did not attack us. A war that will steal from this nation our purpose in both the world and at home. This may be the most important gathering of this party any of us have ever attended. Because from this meeting we will send a message about what we stand. From this meeting we will either emerge as a party divided by war or united in a cause of peace. From this meeting we can emerge either with a new sense of optimism and power, or with a sense of dread and futility.

I am a candidate for the Democratic nomination for president. I am also the cochair of the largest caucus in our party, the Progressive Caucus, and the top Democrat on the oversight subcommittee with jurisdiction over national security. I have led 126 Democrats, nearly two-thirds of the Democratic caucus, to oppose the Iraq resolution.

Iraq was not responsible for the attack on the World Trade Center or the Pentagon. Iraq has not been credibly linked to al-Qaeda's role in 9/11. Iraq was not responsible for the anthrax attack on our nation. Iraq does not have weapons technology to strike this nation. Iraq does not have nuclear weapons. As reported in the *Washington Post,* the CIA says Iraq does not have the intention to attack this nation.

The United Nations inspectors have not been able to prove that Iraq has usable weapons of mass destruction, but if they have any hidden, they are sure to used against our invading troops.

Iraq has been contained before. It can be contained again. Inspections are necessary. War is not. This war is wrong. This war puts the lives of millions of innocent people in Iraq at risk. The administrations battle plan calls for a two-day missile attack on Iraq, a total of 800 missiles are to be aimed at Baghdad, a city of five million. An invasion will follow. This war will put America's moral standing in the world at risk. This war will make America not more safe, but less safe. It will bring more—not less—terror to our shores.

This war will make the entire world less safe and will, like all wars, cause other wars to break out.

This war will put America's sons and daughters at risk for no good reason.

This war illustrates the total bankruptcy of the Bush Administration's policies. A trillion-dollar tax cut for the rich. A trillion dollars for war in Iraq, but no money for the needs of our people.

We are told we have money to blow up cities in Iraq. But no money to rebuild cities in America. We have money to blow up bridges over the Tigris and Euphrates, but no money to build bridges over the Cuyahoga in Cleveland. We have money to retire Saddam Hussein, but no money to protect Social Security. We have money to wage war to ruin the health of the people of Iraq, but no money for a plan which could repair the health of people across America.

Unemployment is up. Foreclosures are up. Wholesale prices are up. The trade deficit is up. And all this administration wants to talk about is war. People are losing their jobs, health care, and retirement security. And all this administration wants to talk about is war. Our state governments can't fund education, or health care or road improvements. And all this administration wants to talk about is war and generate fear. We have stepped into the world of George Orwell where peace is war, where security is control, where bombing innocent people is liberation. This generation didn't travel from the days of duck and cover where we have worked to do away with nuclear weapons to arrive at the days of duct tape and plastic cover where our nation rearms with nuclear weapons to take on the world.

Someone must step forward. Someone must say "Stop." Someone must say America must take a new direction. Someone must say that it is time for a fundamental change of the kind brought by FDR in 1932. We must shake the nation from this color-coded nightmare of terror alerts and attacks on our civil liberties.

We must remind America that its historic mission is not found in dark doctrines of unilateralism and preemption, but in the light of international cooperation for peace and security.

We Democrats must remember who we are. We must remember where we came from. We must sound the trumpet and call all Americans back to the party of the people. We are the party of Lyndon Johnson and the Great Society. We are the party of John F. Kennedy and the New Frontier. We are the party of FDR and the New Deal. We are the party of the people. We are the party whose president faced a broken nation, a nation of people without jobs, without homes, without health care, without retirement security, and he exhorted them to have courage.

Seventy years ago, FDR stood before a fearful nation and said: "We have nothing to fear but fear itself," And he ignited a nation to reaching its promise. It brought one hundred new Democrats into the House. It enabled a sweeping mandate to bring deep, transformational change to our social, economic, and political structure. It remade government for the people. That kind of change is needed today. We can empower a new beginning today. Democrats, I remind you today: We have nothing to fear but fear itself.

Today we need a new faith in America, and in ourselves. Faith that we can change the present condition. Faith that we can regain the confidence, the optimism that the whole world has identified with America. Faith that it is the Democratic party that can once again lead the way to a better day, to a better America, to a better world.

Democrats can move this country forward from a condition of eight million people out of work to a full-employment economy, with a living wage for all. If we believe our party can do this. Let us tell the nation: Yes we can. *Si se puede.*

Democrats can move this country forward from its loss of 3 million good-paying jobs to NAFTA, and we can cancel NAFTA. We can start over and condition trade with America on workers' rights, human rights, and environmental protection. Yes we can. *Si se puede.*

Democrats can move this country forward from 40,000,000 without health insurance to a single-payer system which provides quality health care for all. Yes we can. *Si se puede.*

Democrats can move this county forward from underfunded schools, underpaid teachers, and undereducated youths to making education our top funding priority and providing free college education for all.

Democrats can move this country forward from a condition where our air, our water, and our land is being ruined by multinational corporate interests to a place where we demonstrate that environmental protection is our path to sustaining the life of the planet. Yes we can. *Si se puede.*

Democrats can move this country forward from the destructive Patriot Act to restore for Americans the right to assemble, the right to free speech, to right to be free in our persons from unreasonable search and seizure. Yes we can. *Si se puede.*

Just as FDR proclaimed his Four Freedoms, it is time for us to reclaim our freedoms and mission as the party of the people, with a declaration of the human economic rights of the American people.

> We have a right to a job.
> We have a right to quality health care.
> We have a right to a good education.
> We have a right to decent housing.
> We have a right to food fit to eat.
> We have a right to water fit to drink.
> We have a right to be free from fear.
> We have a right to be free from war.
> We have a right to be human.

In the months ahead, I will travel this nation with this message. I will ask for your support and, if I am the nominee of this party, together we will lead this party to victory, this nation to greatness, this world to peace. Thank you and let us call on God to bless and keep this country.

Adapted from a speech to the Democratic National Committee, February 22, 2003, Washington, DC.

INNER SPACE

One of the *Columbia* astronauts, Kalpana Chawla, is said to have looked upon the earth from the silence of outer space and said to fellow voyagers: "Look! The whole world is reflected in the retina of my eye." As she watched the whole world, the whole world is watching us to see what is reflected in our eyes—the light of peace or the fires of war. We who gather carry a vision of peace. We see the world as one. We carry a vision of human unity. We see the world undivided. Today and tomorrow we act on that vision.

To those leaders in our country struggling in inner space, those who have war in their eyes and in their hearts and would project it upon the world: The whole world is watching. "Look, the whole world is reflected in the retina of my eye." America is reflected in the irises of a billions of eyes. The whole world is watching to see if the power of our morality is greater than the power which would unleash our weapons. Peaceful coexistence or war. The whole world is watching. A fist or an open hand. The whole world is watching. First use of nuclear weapons or leadership in global disarmament. The whole world is watching. Bombs or bread to the Iraqi people, to the Iranian people, to the North Korean people. The whole world is watching.

Some in the name of peace, prepare us for war, in the name of liberty, prepare us for submission, in the name courage, prepare us to be fearful. Let all Americans challenge war, submission and fear! Some power has ruled there is no permit to march today. Yet we are on the march. The direction of peace is forward! We are on the march. The direction of human unity is forward! We are on the march. The direction of political change is forward. We are on the march. We will either bring an end to war or we will bring an end to a war-like administration. We are on the march!

Two hundred and fourteen years ago the First Congress standing upon the holy ground of a new Constitution met in this city. Their permit came from the Declaration of Independence. The same high power which entrusted them entrusts us with the Declaration, the Constitution, and the Bill of Rights. We call upon the Spirit of the Founders to guide us as we create a new world where all may live in peace.

The United States, brought forth by the power of human unity, seeks to be reborn. We invoke the Spirit of Freedom. We hear the cadence of courage echo across the ages: "Life, Liberty, pursuit of Happiness." Once again, the hour has come for us to stand for unity, even as our government tells us we must follow it into war. Once again the hour has come for us to be strong of heart. The direction of human unity is forward. We are on the march. It is our government which must follow, or be swept aside.

Speech read from Dennis Kucinich's Palm Pilot in New York City, February 15, 2003.